THINKING SPANISH TEACHERS' HANDBOOK

TITLES OF RELATED INTEREST

Thinking Translation: A Course in Translation Method: French to English
Sándor Hervey and Ian Higgins

In Other Words: A Coursebook on Translation
Mona Baker

Redefining Translation
Lance Hewson and Jacky Martin

Translation Studies
Susan Bassnett

Colloquial Spanish
Untza Otaola Alday

Colloquial Spanish of Latin America
Roberto Rodríguez-Saona

Manual of Business Spanish
Michael Gorman and María-Luisa Henson

Spanish Business Situations
Michael Gorman and María-Luisa Henson

The Linguistics Encyclopedia
Kirsten Malmkjær, ed.

THINKING SPANISH TRANSLATION
TEACHERS' HANDBOOK

Sándor Hervey, Ian Higgins
and
Louise M. Haywood

London and New York

First published in 1996
by Routledge
11 New Fetter Lane, London EC4P 4EE

Simultaneously published in the USA and Canada
by Routledge
29 West 35th Street, New York, NY 10001

© 1996 Sándor Hervey, Ian Higgins and Louise M. Haywood

The authors assert the moral right to be
identified as the authors of this work.

Typeset in Times by Michael Mepham, Frome, Somerset
Printed and bound in Great Britain by
TJ Press (Padstow) Ltd, Padstow, Cornwall

All rights reserved. No part of this book may be reprinted or
reproduced or utilized in any form or by any electronic, mechanical
or other means, now known or hereafter invented, including
photocopying and recording, or in any information storage or
retrieval system, without permission in writing from the publishers.

British Library Cataloguing in Publication Data
A catalogue record for this book is available from the British Library

Library of Congress Cataloguing in Publication Data
A catalogue record for this book has been requested

ISBN 0–415–12606–1 book
ISBN 0–415–12607–X cassette
ISBN 0–415–12608–8 book and cassette pack

Contents

Introduction	*page* 1
Practical 1	
Notes for tutors	8
1.2 Gist translation	10
Practical 2	
Notes for tutors	12
2.1 Commentary on translation of the extract from 'Estación de la mano'	14
2.2 Speed translation	18
Practical 3	
Notes for tutors	20
3.2 Commentary on the extract from *Señas de identidad*	22
Practical 4	
Notes for tutors	26
4.1 Commentary on the extract from 'La golondrina'	28
4.3 Published TT of 'Toco tu boca...'	32
Practical 5	
Notes for tutors	34
5.1 Commentary on the extract from *Reivindicación del conde don Julián*	36
5.2 Commentary on the extract from *Tiempo de silencio*	38
Practical 6	
Notes for tutors	45
6.1 Commentary on the extract from *Del sentimiento trágico de la vida*	46
6.2 Speed translation	48
Practical 7	
Notes for tutors	51
7.1 Commentary on literal meaning in the extract from *The Life of Saint Teresa of Avila*	52
7.2 Speed translation	56

Practical 8
    Notes for tutors   59
    8.1   Commentary on connotative meanings in the extract from *Yerma*   60
    8.2   Commentary on connotative meanings in 'Sinfonía en gris mayor'   64

Practical 9
    Notes for tutors   70
    9.1   Transcript of taped extract 'El susto más grande...'   72
          Standard version of taped extract 'El susto más grande...'   73

Practical 10
    Notes for tutors   74
    10.1   Commentary on language variety in the extract from *La vida es sueño*   76
    10.2   Transcript of taped extract '¿Cómo se distingue..?'   82

Practical 11
    Notes for tutors   84
    11.1   Song-lyric assignment: 'Gracias a la vida'   86

Practical 12
    Notes for tutors   88
    12.2   Speed translation   90

Practical 13
    Notes for tutors   93
    13.1   Published translation of the archaeological abstract   94
    13.2   Translation of the extract from the 'Congelación' text   95
    13.3   Published translation of the spectroscopy abstract   96

Practical 14
    Notes for tutors   98

Practical 15
    Notes for tutors   101
    15.2   ST of the extract from *Colombia: país de Eldorado*   102

Practicals 16–19
    Notes for tutors   104

Introduction

Variety is the spice of life. In the coursebook which this handbook accompanies we have attempted to provide variety in a number of ways. In the first place, our approach is based on constantly drawing attention to the range of textual features (textual variables) that, in different proportions, make up the overall effects of particular texts. The progression through a series of topics important to translation, discussed in individual chapters and examined in accompanying practicals, treats this variety of textual features and levels of textual feature in sequence.

In the second place, we consider it vital for students to be made thoroughly aware of the variety of purposes, needs and practical situations that target texts (TTs) can serve, both in principle and in practice, according to such variables as: the amount of time available to the translator, the stipulated requirements of paymasters, the explicit or tacit needs and tastes of a putative audience for the TT, the availability of reference works, and so on. While it is impossible to reproduce in the classroom the real conditions governing this variety of purposes and circumstances, we urge tutors using this course to make every effort to stipulate such conditions for each of the practical translation tasks they set, and to encourage students to keep stipulated tasks and purposes firmly in mind when producing their TTs. In a sense, the best one can hope to do in a classroom situation is to simulate 'real' translation work by what amounts to a form of role-playing, whereby students imagine that a particular TT needs to be produced in order to fulfil certain carefully defined requirements (for example, publication in a particular journal or magazine, subtitling a documentary for Channel 4, or production on stage at a particular theatre). The tutor's ingenuity in devising and circumscribing suitable, though imaginary, translation situations is a welcome contribution towards a lively implementation of the course, and is also likely to sustain student interest.

In the third place, a glance at the contents list suffices to show another aspect of variety evident in the course: in terms of the textual genres used in practicals at various points in the course. This variety is not only pedagogically sound, in that it familiarizes students with the different kinds of translation problem that diverse genres of texts (for example, literary translation or technical translation) are likely to present, but it also enhances and sustains, as we have found in teaching the course, the interest that students take both in practical work and in theoretical discussion.

Finally, we recommend that course tutors vary their *modus operandi*. While some practicals are best conducted on the basis of individual TTs produced by students, submitted in advance of the class and gone over in general tutor-led discussion, other practicals are suitable for students working in small groups, either in the classroom or at home. Small groups may either be asked to discuss particular passages and to report back to the class at large, or to collaborate on TTs and commentaries that can be presented for subsequent discussion by the tutor and the class as a whole. Furthermore, in some cases, either individual students or small groups can be set tasks other than producing a TT from scratch. They may, for instance, be asked to evaluate a published translation, or to edit an unfinished TT. Using diverse forms of classroom activity is, again, not only sound pedagogic practice, maximizing the amount that students can learn from interaction with each other as well as with the tutor, but also, by varying the pace of proceedings in practicals, it cuts down the danger of classroom tedium.

In what follows, we have attempted to include, chapter by chapter and practical by practical, various hints and suggestions to tutors for the conduct of classroom sessions, together with sample texts and commentaries from which tutors can gain a clear idea of what they can hope to get out of each practical session. It is, of course, up to the individual judgement of tutors whether they wish to use our sample texts (for example, by handing out duplicate copies to students at a suitable point in the practical), or whether they wish to modify these or replace them with their own versions.

Whether, and how, the completed exercises are assessed will depend on the assessment system used in a given institution. In our teaching of the course, we have put more emphasis on discovery and learning than on testing; it is, in any case, difficult to include group work in individual assessment. Nevertheless, students do like feedback on how well they are doing, and there is no reason why some or all of the exercises done individually should not be graded. Even if no mark is given, it is important that work handed in should be returned fully commented on. If the tutor plays the role of *rapporteur* when returning work in class, the amount of annotation required on each script is reduced.

As with any course, no two classes on the same topic follow the same pattern or go at the same rate. In full awareness of this element of unpredictability, we have provided a tentative schema for the course, based on a weekly two-hour class and a fortnightly home exercise (see pp. 4–7). This pattern can, of course, be varied *ad lib.*, with other exercises substituted for the ones given. Again, local conditions and individual tutors' experience will be the determining factors. In any case, Chapters 16–19 have a twofold 'wild card' value: first, they can be used at whatever points in the course the tutor thinks fit, and second, they do not usually need a full two hours of class time. They can, therefore, be useful in correcting the effects of unforeseen disruptions to whatever scheme the tutor has decided on. Timetable and student workload permitting, it is worth considering devoting three hours per week, rather than two, to each unit. With this pattern, the first hour can be devoted to discussion of the issues and examples contained in a given chapter, and, later on in the week, a whole two-hour class to the corresponding practical.

Finally, a note on examining. Proficiency at the end of the course can be examined in a number of ways. A possible format is that of a three-hour paper containing two questions. The first assignment is an evaluation of a given English TT (printed opposite the ST). In this assignment, candidates are asked to give their own edited TT at all points where they are critical of the one they are evaluating. The second assignment is to translate into English a text different from the first in either genre or language variety or both. The candidate's TT is preceded by a short discussion of strategic decisions related to translating the ST, and followed by notes on the candidate's salient decisions of detail. Both assignments are formulated in terms familiar from practicals. For both, sufficient contextual information is provided for all the major translation problems to be clear. We have found that, if there is to be enough time for analytical comment, the texts set have to be rather short – not more than 100–120 words, depending on the passage. If the examination timetable permitted, a less frantic and more satisfying format would be to give each assignment a three-hour slot, or even to schedule a whole day for the complete test.

Given the limitations of a three-hour examination paper, a more satisfying possibility is for assessment to be carried out by means of a dissertation or a portfolio. A possible option is to examine students in a 2,000–3,000 word dissertation (containing a TT together with commentary), candidates being allowed about eight weeks for the task. This time-scale makes it possible for students to make their choice from a wider range of STs differing in genre and language variety. It also gives students an opportunity to work on an ST of a more satisfying size, such as, say, an article or a chapter from a book – but in this case the dissertation needs to be 10,000–12,000 words long; consequently, where student numbers are high, the sheer weight of marking will make this an impracticable solution. The option of a portfolio – again, if tutor workload does not make marking prohibitive – has the advantage of combining an element of continuous assessment (where a portfolio of, say, three 2,000–3,000-word, or six 1,000-word, pieces of translation and commentary is completed over the duration of the course) with giving students the opportunity to try their hand at a selection of STs drawn from a variety of genres and registers.

As the rationale of the course implies, we expect candidates to use in their examination the reference books they use in all their practical work: a Spanish–English dictionary such as the 1992 *Collins Spanish Dictionary* or *The Oxford Spanish Dictionary* (1994), a monolingual Spanish dictionary (we recommend the 1975 María Moliner *Diccionario de uso del Español*), an English dictionary (preferably the *Collins Concise English Dictionary*, 1992 edition) and a thesaurus. (Under examination conditions the use of a greater number of reference books than these tends to be counter-productive. Glosses for the meanings of expressions not found in the three basic reference works named, and not easily deducible from the context, should be supplied in the examination papers.) To produce reasonable working conditions, each examination candidate should ideally sit at a double desk or a small table, or share a larger table with a candidate sitting diagonally opposite – it is important to provide candidates with space to spread out their papers and reference books.

We close this introduction with the reminder that, in our view, any rational and methodical approach to translation – no matter what particular theoretical line it may pursue – is better than a purely hit-and-miss, naive and intuitive approach. We offer this course with confidence, borne out over many years of experience, in the benefits of approaching translation in a self-aware, analytic and methodical frame of mind.

N.B. (1) The oral texts for use in practicals are available on a cassette: S. Hervey, I. Higgins and L. M. Haywood, *Thinking Spanish Translation*, obtainable from Routledge Ltd., ITPS, Cheriton House, North Way, Andover, Hants SP10 5BE, or from Routledge Inc., 29 West 35th Street, New York, NY 10001, USA.

(2) Users of the course are assured that all the publishers concerned have permitted us to authorize hereby, gratis, the photocopying of any of the material in this handbook, as long as it is for distribution to students for instructional use and is not sold for profit.

Sándor Hervey
Ian Higgins
Louise M. Haywood

SPECIMEN SCHEMA OF COURSE

Note

(a) The term 'marked' implies appropriately detailed comments on work handed in by students in advance of the class, regardless of whether the work is given a mark or grade.
(b) The term 'set' implies: first, briefly explaining the point and the requirements of a home assignment; and second, making clear arrangements for students to hand in the completed assignment.

This schema is based on one two-hour class per week.

Unit 1

(Set preliminary home assignment at start of session, in advance of the first practical.)

(i) Discuss Chapter 1.
(ii) Discuss marked home assignment: extract from the Book of Genesis.
(iii) Gist translation: extract from *ABC*, 9 January 1993.
(iv) Set home exercise: Cortázar, 'Estación de la mano'.

Introduction

Unit 2

(i) Discuss Chapter 2.
(ii) Discuss marked home assignment: 'Estación de la mano'.
(iii) Speed translation: 'Haití '.

Unit 3

(i) Discuss Chapter 3.
(ii) Do assignment on 'Parque Tecnológico' (individually or in groups).
(iii) Do assignment on *Señas de identidad* (in groups).
(iv) Do assignment on 'Elecciones Locales'.
(v) Set home assignment: extract from 'La golondrina'.

Unit 4

(i) Discuss Chapter 4.
(ii) Discuss marked home assignment: extract from 'La golondrina'.
(iii) Do assignment on 'Paisaje plástico'.
(iv) Do assignment on 'Toco tu boca...' (individually or in groups).

Unit 5

(i) Discuss Chapter 5.
(ii) Do assignment on extract from *Reivindicación del conde don Julián*.
(iii) Do assignment on extract from *Tiempo de silencio*.
(iv) Set assignment: extract from *Del sentimiento trágico de la vida*.

Unit 6

(i) Discuss Chapter 6.
(ii) Discuss marked home assignment: extract from *Del sentimiento trágico de la vida*.
(iii) Speed translation: Conference Poster.

Unit 7

(i) Discuss Chapter 7.
(ii) Do assignment on extract from *The Life of Saint Teresa of Avila*.
(iii) Speed translation: Encyclopedia entry.
(iv) Set home assignment: Darío, 'Sinfonía en gris mayor'.

Unit 8

(i) Discuss Chapter 8.
(ii) Discuss marked home assignment: Darío, 'Sinfonía en gris mayor'.
(iii) Do assignment on extract from Lorca, *Yerma*.

Unit 9

(i) Discuss Chapter 9.
(ii) Do assignment on taped extract: 'El susto más grande...'
(iii) Do assignment on extract from Pereda, *Sotileza*.
(iv) Set home assignment: Calderón, *La vida es sueño*.

Unit 10

(i) Discuss Chapter 10.
(ii) Discuss marked home assignment: Calderón, *La vida es sueño*.
(iii) Discuss taped extracts transcribed in coursebook.
(iv) Do voice-over assignment on taped extract: '¿Cómo se distingue...?'

Unit 11

(i) Discuss Chapter 11.
(ii) Do assignment on extract from travel brochure (individually or in groups).
(iii) Start assignment on 'Gracias a la vida', for completion at home.

Unit 12

(i) Discuss Chapter 12.
(ii) Discuss marked home assignment: 'Gracias a la vida'.
(iii) Do subtitling assignment: extract from *Viridiana*.
(iv) Speed translation: 'Sorpresa: Luis Pérez, titular'.

Unit 13

(i) Discuss Chapter 13.
(ii) Do assignment on archaeology abstract.
(iii) Do assignment on 'Congelación' extract.
(iv) Do assignment on spectroscopy abstract.
(v) Set home assignment: 'Fish steaks in green sauce' recipes.

Introduction

Unit 14

(i) Discuss Chapter 14.
(ii) Discuss marked home assignment: 'Fish steaks in green sauce' recipes.
(iii) Do assignment on 'Brazo de gitano' recipe.
(iv) Do assignment on extract from *Santo Domingo Tours*.

NB Exercise (iv) is actually best done at home, if this can be fitted into an acceptable work-schedule of home assignments.

Unit 15

(i) Discuss Chapter 15.
(ii) (If applicable) Discuss marked home assignment: extract from *Santo Domingo Tours*.
(iii) Do assignment on the passages on p. 183 of the coursebook.
(iv) Do assignment on extract from *Colombia: país de Eldorado*.

Units 16–19

To be fitted in at the tutor's convenience.

Practical 1

NOTES FOR TUTORS

1.1 Intralingual translation

This exercise makes a good introduction to the course, and ideally should be done at home – with each student working individually – and handed in for marking before Practical 1.

Tutors will probably find that many of the students opt for adapting the text for a Sunday School lesson. Many will be rather imprecise in specifying their putative audience – the age-range, denomination and social and regional background of the children are often not given. It is also unusual to find explicit mention of whether the rephrased text is meant for silent reading, reading aloud, dramatized reading or 'spontaneous' oral narrative. Yet all these considerations are crucial to a strategic approach and to assessing the success of the student texts.

Another common approach is to render the Genesis story in the form of a pastiche (for example, told in the manner of a news report). In such a case, students generally fail to recognize (and explain) that their text is actually for a fairly sophisticated adult readership (or audience, in the case of oral performance) for whom the rephrased text serves the purpose of a sketch or skit designed to entertain, and perhaps to have a satirical edge. Where the pastiche is satirical, students are sometimes confused about who or what is the target of the satire.

Questions of hidden ideology – the basic religious, philosophical, moral or political attitude one takes to the original Genesis story – play an important, but often overlooked, role in how the story is recast.

It is, therefore, a good idea, at this early stage of the course, to stress the importance of developing a *strategy* of TT formulation by, among other things, being explicitly aware of such considerations as the precise purpose of the text, the audience at which it is aimed, and the channel and medium in which it is realized.

Practical 1

1.2 Gist translation

The text given on pp. 10–11 may be reproduced and handed out for work in class after discussion of the Genesis assignment has been completed.

This assignment serves a double purpose: putting students in a situation where they need to complete a TT under pressure of a strict time limit, and illustrating a particular type of translation task that professional translators may be faced with, namely producing a TT that is a précis of the salient points contained in the ST. Tutors should emphasize to students that time will not allow a word-by-word, sentence-by-sentence approach to their task: they must aim at producing a short English text that, without becoming telegraphic, condenses the contents of the ST into a few lines. In our experience, many students apply their habitual translation techniques to this assignment and end up with a faithful rendering of a fraction of the ST, thereby failing to carry out the assignment set. It is helpful to warn them of this danger in advance.

We have also found that, in summarizing the contents of a ST, students often ignore the role of textual features in the ST whose function is to qualify the attitudes of the writer, to attribute views to particular sources, or to indicate the reliability of particular assertions. As these qualifications have a vital thematic function in newspaper reportage, it is important to convey their impact in the TT. Doing this would, of course, present no difficulty in a faithful translation of the ST. However, in a gist translation one would almost certainly need to signal these features by means other than those used in the ST (that is, through compensation in kind).

It is helpful for the tutor to produce a simple gist translation which can be compared with student versions and used in discussion of the difficulties and solutions presented by the assignment. Students may also find it useful if the tutor discusses in advance the choice of the television or radio channel on which the news bulletin is to be broadcast.

PRACTICAL 1

1.2 GIST TRANSLATION

Assignment

Produce, in fifteen minutes, a gist translation of the following passage suitable for use as a news bulletin on television or radio.

Contextual information

The text (438 words) is a report from the 9 January 1993 issue of the Spanish newspaper *ABC*.

Practical 1

Text

EL GOBIERNO PIDE MODERACIÓN EN LAS SUBIDAS SALARIALES PARA MANTENER EL EMPLEO INDUSTRIAL

Madrid. P.R.M.

El empleo industrial cayó hasta marzo un 3,1 por 100, con lo que vuelve a la situación de mediados de 1991, el peor año de la crisis del empleo en la industria, según aseguró ayer el secretario de Estado de Industria. Según Alvaro Espina la industria necesita una reducción de los costes laborales y de los salarios para ser más competitiva.

Alvaro Espina hizo públicos ayer los resultados que elabora Industria sobre productividad industrial del tercer trimestre y adelantó las previsiones para todo el año 1992.

Según estos datos, el Indice de Producción Industrial cayó para el conjunto del año un 0,6 por 100, descenso menor que el año anterior debido a la arrancada en falso del primer trimestre del año, donde se mantuvo unas tasas positivas del 2,2 por 100.

Sin embargo, la productividad, principal indicador del clima industrial, ha experimentado un crecimiento del 3,2 por 100. Esta cifra, no se corresponde a anteriores estadísticas trimestrales, debido que ahora para su cálculo se ha añadido un nuevo indicador, el valor añadido industrial bruto (VAB), que ha sido para todo 1992 de 1,2 por 100. Esto, unido a un descenso del empleo del 1,9 por 100 para todo el año ha provocado el crecimiento de la productividad.

El secretario de Estado alertó sobre los desequilibrios entre los costes laborales, que crecieron un 3,4 por 100, y los precios en la industria, que han crecido tan sólo un 1,4 por 100, manteniendo un ritmo parecido al de el resto de la Comunidad Europea. Este desequilibrio se eleva a un 15 por 100 desde 1989, lo que, a juicio del Ministerio, es una de las causas de la crisis por la que atraviesa actualmente la industria.

Las empresas, según Alvaro Espina, se han visto obligadas a soportar esta diferencia en su cuenta de resultados, lo que ha provocado 'el descenso de beneficios o aumento de las pérdidas'.

Con respecto al futuro, no se espera que los precios industriales se incrementen a un ritmo superior al 2 por 100 anuales, por lo que Industria considera que para corregir este desequilibrio habrá que ajustar los costes para conseguir una mayor competitividad.

Industria considera que en 1993 no es previsible que mejore sustancialmente la producción, y que tampoco se podrá recuperar el equilibrio con un ritmo fuerte de productividad, como en épocas anteriores, lo que incidiría en más pérdida de empleo.

Reprinted by kind permission from *ABC*, sábado 9 de enero de 1993, copyright © El País International, S.A.

Practical 2

NOTES FOR TUTORS

2.1 Strategic decisions and decisions of detail; translation loss

This assignment is best done at home, with each student working individually. It can then be handed in and marked in time for discussion in Practical 2. The essence of the assignment should be clear from the commentary and TT printed on pp. 14–17. These are provided both as a sample layout for this type of assignment (although endnotes are more practical than footnotes for most students), and as a reminder to call students' attention to a number of general considerations.

First, this practical offers a platform for clarifying and stressing both the distinction between *strategy* and *decisions of detail*, and the important link between them (that is, decisions of detail in the TT should be guided by one's strategic approach to translating a given ST).

Second, the TT we offer here will doubtless differ from student versions, as well as from the tutor's own preferred solutions. This presents an opportunity for stressing the fact that there can be no *definitive* translation of a given ST, only more or less plausible and more or less felicitous attempts at translation.

Finally, this assignment offers an early opportunity to insist on the importance of context both as a crucial factor in determining strategy and, often, as the sole basis for making decisions of detail. For instance, the rendering of 'Yo encendía entonces un brasero' in line 14 of the ST has to be weighed up in the light of the historical context of the story: is the object likely to be an electric heater? Similarly, the force of the 'naturalmente' in 'Naturalmente, modeló una mano' (line 19) is all too easily overlooked and mistranslated, unless the translator is absolutely clear about the fact that Dg is actually a disembodied hand. Even more importantly, the entire interpretation of the extract is dependent upon this bizarre fact, a piece of contextual information which does not become explicit until the second paragraph of the narrative ('Todas las tardes volvía la mano...', line 11). Students do occasionally overlook, or refuse to believe, this piece of information. An important implication for the tutor is that, when setting assignments, great care is needed in formulating the contextual information supplied along with the ST. In this particular instance, tutors may choose to set contextual research as part of the assignment for students – the risk is that a majority of students will fall far short of completing this part of the assignment satisfactorily.

2.2 Speed translation

McCluskey (1987, p. 18) stresses that most undergraduate courses leave students seriously unprepared for combining speed with accuracy, as they would be required to do if earning their living as translators. In this course, therefore, we have included the occasional 'speed translation' to be done in class. This one retains an element of gist translation (see Practical 1), and introduces a word limit as well as a time limit. Unless students sift out circumstantial detail, they will almost certainly fail to meet either limit. The text as given here may be reproduced for handing out in class when discussion of the 'Estación de la mano' assignment has been completed.

PRACTICAL 2

2.1 Strategic decisions and decisions of detail; translation loss

COMMENTARY ON TRANSLATION OF THE EXTRACT FROM 'ESTACIÓN DE LA MANO'

(i) Strategic problems

In general terms, the salient strategic problems presented by this ST derive from a narrative style woven out of a combination of ordinary, literary, and 'scientific' features.

In short, 'Estación de la mano' is a bizarre tale told in a mixture of literary and matter-of-fact terms. Creating a balanced TT that retains the alternately literary, mundane, and quasi-scientific presentation of events (see, for instance, the contrast between 'semanas teñidas de luces violetas', 'Todas las tardes volvía la mano', and 'mi interés se tornó bien pronto analítico'), yet manages to sustain for the benefit of the English-speaking reader the ST's air of quiet mystery and suspense, is a major strategic difficulty and concern. To lose the literary aspects of the ST would be to reduce the TT to a flat, colourless text (which the ST certainly is not); to fail to achieve sufficient reticence is to risk reducing the TT to a piece of over-worked bombastic trash (which, again, is not true of the ST). In short, the major strategic consideration must be to aim at a TT that can be plausibly read in English as a subtle and masterly 'tale of the unexpected'.

One textual feature that requires special attention is the time-reference of the narrative. While we do not recommend making the TT into a pastiche of, say, the English of H. G. Wells, it is certainly a good idea, in the light of the somewhat Wellsian flavour of the ST, for the TT to contain some sparingly used elements of vocabulary and syntax with a mildly archaic character. Our preferred strategy would be to avoid excessively modern colloquialisms.

Another important textual feature, one that is likely to create immediate translation problems, hinges on the element of suspense in the extract: in particular its mixture of mundane matter-of-factness and of the bizarre and supernatural. Care is needed in the TT to make the mixture a subtle one, not to give away too much too

Practical 2

soon (for instance, by revealing that Dg is really a disembodied hand in paragraph 1, rather than further on in paragraph 2), and not to be too explicit: thus leaving the reader a degree of dramatic uncertainty about the nature of the events described. In this connection, the use of anaphora creates strategic difficulties throughout the text. Because of grammatical gender in Spanish ('la mano'), the ST uses feminine reference to Dg throughout: however, to use 'she' throughout the TT would be to overmark the gender characteristics of an essentially genderless creature. A possible strategic solution, which we adopt in our TT, is to use anaphoric 'It' in paragraph 1 (thereby keeping a genderless reference to the as yet unexplained creature, and marking its mysterious nature by using a capital letter), to change to anaphoric 'she' for paragraph 2 (in token of the narrator's changed attitude to one of cosy companionship, as though Dg were a pet or a comfortable female companion), and to revert to anaphoric 'it', but this time with a lower case initial, for paragraph 3 (where the narrator's attitude has changed to seeing Dg as an object of scientific interest).

(ii)   TT and commentary on decisions of detail

I invented names for It: the one I liked best was Dg, because this was a name one could only think, but not say.[1] I tried to arouse Its suspected[2] vanity by leaving rings and bracelets lying around on the shelves, while in secret I observed Its reaction constantly.[3] On one occasion I thought It was about to put on[4] the jewels, but It turned out to be merely examining them, circling round and round without touching them, just like a mistrustful spider.[5] Once It did actually

1   The TT departs from literal translation by expanding the rendering of 'un nombre que sólo se dejaba pensar' by adding 'but not say', without which the TT would be incomprehensible. The alternatives 'a name which can only be thought', or 'a name which one can only think' are almost ungrammatical, and are certainly obscure: the point made in the ST (which is the suitability of an unpronounceable name for an extraordinary creature) has to be made more explicit in the TT if it is to be grasped.

2   The more literal meaning of 'probable' is inappropriate to the context: the point is not that the creature's vanity is objectively probable, but that the narrator thinks it might be vain.

3   The more literal 'with secret constancy/persistence' has been rejected as translationese. Our solution involves substantial grammatical transposition: the adjective 'secreta' is transposed to the adverbial complement 'in secret' and the noun 'constancia' to the adverb 'constantly'.

4   The more literal rendering 'adorn itself with' is rejected as translationese: despite the resulting translation loss (see in particular the connection between 'se adornaría' and 'su probable vanidad') the more neutral and colourless 'put on' is preferable.

5   The aptness of the simile is not fully appreciated until the subsequent context reveals that Dg is really a disembodied hand; it is all the more important to ensure that the image of the spider-like movements is clearly conveyed in the TT.

venture to put on an amethyst ring, though only for an instant, discarding it immediately as if it were red hot.[6] After that, I quickly hid the jewels while It was away, and from then on I had the impression that It was much happier.

Thus[7] the seasons came and went, some gracefully, others in weeks tinted with a violet hue,[8] without disturbing our cosy routine. Every afternoon the hand would arrive, often wet with the autumn rain, and I would see her[9] lying spreadeagled on the carpet, meticulously drying one finger with another, and making small jerking movements of apparent contentment.[10] On cold evenings her shadow would take on a violet tinge.[11] Then I would light a brazier[12] at my feet and she would cuddle up to it, only stirring halfheartedly[13] to accept an album of pictures to leaf through, or a ball of wool which she enjoyed twisting and tangling. She was, as I soon learned, incapable of staying still for long. One day she came across a trough full of clay which she fell upon avidly; for hours and hours she went on moulding the clay while I, with my back to her, pretended

6   Using the phrase 'red hot', besides being idiomatic in context, avoids the need for further repetition of anaphoric 'it'; had we not used 'It' for denoting Dg, this sentence would have become both cumbersome and potentially confusing as a result of too many occurrences of 'it', some referring to Dg and some to the amethyst ring.

7   The degree of 'purple style' in this sentence justifies the use of the more formal connective 'thus', in preference to a more colloquial alternative such as 'So...'.

8   The more literally exact 'tinged/tinted with violet lights', while retaining the 'purple' style of the ST, is felt to be unidiomatic to the point of translationese: 'with a violet hue' retains the literary flavour of the ST without jeopardizing TL idiomaticity.

9   The shift to anaphoric 'she' signals a change in the narrator's attitude to Dg during this period of 'cosy routine' (see strategic comments).

10 In describing the details of Dg's behaviour literal faithfulness to the ST is far less important than finding plausible ways of recreating in the TT the appropriate visual images: implicitly, the creature is described as behaving like a pet, but there is a reminder of its unusual nature in 'secarse prolijamente un dedo con otro'.

11 This phrase partially echoes the earlier 'teñidas de luces violetas': in order not to make the TT excessively repetitious, the alternative 'tinge' not taken up earlier is brought in to replace 'hue'.

12 The reference is to a small charcoal heater of the kind often used in Spanish households. The object itself is culturally alien to the Anglo-Saxon reader, and no serious translation loss would have resulted from describing it simply as 'a stove'; the cultural strangeness of 'a brazier' merely injects a slight degree of exoticism into the TT, which helps to distance the narrative from ordinary experience.

13 The choice of 'halfheartedly' represents a literally inexact, but idiomatically justified and contextually apt rendering of 'displicente'.

Practical 2

not to notice what she was doing.[14] Not unexpectedly, she had sculpted[15] a hand. I let it dry and placed it on my desk to show that I liked it. This turned out to be a mistake: looking at[16] her rigid and somewhat distorted self-portrait soon came to irritate her. When I hid the object,[17] she tactfully pretended not to have noticed.

Soon my interest in the hand became analytical. Tired of treating it[18] as an object of wonder, I now wanted to *know*, which[19] always spells the inevitable and fateful end to all adventures. I was plagued by questions about my strange guest: did it grow? could it feel? could it understand? did it love?[20] I set up tests and devised experiments. I had found out that the hand could read, and yet never wrote. One afternoon, I opened the window and placed a pen and some blank sheets of paper on the table, and when Dg came in I withdrew so as not to disturb the timid creature. Through the keyhole I observed it as it did its usual rounds of the room; then, hesitantly, it approached the desk and took up the pen. I heard the scratching of the nib, and after an uneasy wait I entered the study. Diagonally across the page, penned in a neat hand, it had written: 'This resolution cancels all previous instructions until further notice.'[21] I could never induce it to write again.

14   There is a substantial grammatical transposition in this solution, in order to avoid unidiomatic nominal constructions in the TT: formulations like 'pretended not to be preoccupied with its activity' would be conspicuous translationese.

15   Tense causes a problem of detail in the TT: in the context, 'sculpted', 'was sculpting' and 'had sculpted' are all plausible alternatives. We choose 'had sculpted' in order to pick up the narrative at the point when the sculpture was finished.

16   The grammatical transposition (in particular the avoidance of an abstract nominal 'contemplation') necessary for producing an idiomatic rendering further suggests that 'contemplating' is too formal and pedantic in the context: we chose to replace it by the more neutral and colloquial 'looking at'.

17   Although anaphoric 'it' could be used here, the TT becomes clearer and more felicitous through the insertion of 'the object', in particular through the contextually apt collocative echo of the cliché 'the offending object'.

18   The shift to anaphoric 'it' signals yet another change in the narrator's attitude to Dg: this time to treating it as an object of scientific curiosity (see strategic comments).

19   With the aid of punctuation the TT can be correctly construed as meaning that the quest for analytical knowledge invariably puts an end to the romance of adventure. This construal is not immediately obvious in the ST, which, if the function of the comma after 'saber' is ignored, can be easily misconstrued by interpreting 'invariable y funesto fin de toda aventura' as the grammatical object of 'saber'.

20   The variation between 'did it' and 'could it' is justified purely by reasons of collocational felicity in English.

21   Communicative translation is appropriate here: the written message must read like a plausible official memo in English, hence the use of bureaucratic jargon in our TT.

PRACTICAL 2

2.2 SPEED TRANSLATION

Assignment

Produce, in 15 minutes, a 125-word article in English based on the text below, paying due attention to the choice of an appropriate style.

Contextual information

The text is a 169-word item, giving general information on Haiti, taken from one of the Banco Exterior de España's economic reports *Estudios de países 3/1987*.

Text

HAITÍ

El tercio occidental de la isla La Española (27.750 km²) y las pequeñas islas Gonave, Tortuga y otras constituyen el estado haitiano; Haití es el nombre que los indígenas daban a su isla. La población, 6,5 milliones de habitantes, es negra y mulata prácticamente en su totalidad.

El idioma oficial es el francés, pero se habla el 'créole' y 'patois', mezcla de francés antiguo, lenguas africanas y algo de español. La religión mayoritaria es el vudú, subdividida en varias sociedades secretas, según su origen: Bizango (Bisau), etc. El catolicismo, derivado del colonialismo francés, y el protestantismo, de la ocupación e influencia norteamericanas, juegan un importante papel en la alfabetización del país. La West Indies Mission y la American Baptists Home Missionary Society han constituido en Haití la comunidad protestante relativamente más numerosa de Latinoamérica.

Practical 2

La dictadura hereditaria de los Duvalier (1957) fue derrocada en 1986. Haití se halla en una etapa política provisional, en transición hacia un sistema democrático.

La capital del estado es Puerto Príncipe.

> Reprinted from *Extebank: Estudios de países 3/87; República Dominicana/Haití* (Madrid: Banco Exterior de España, March, 1987), copyright © Servicio de Estudios Económicos, Banco Exterior de España.

Practical 3

NOTES FOR TUTORS

3.1 Cultural transposition; compensation

This assignment lends itself equally well to individual or group work in class. Much could be said about the ST and the TT in the subsequent class discussion, but the tutor should make sure that attention is focused on cultural transposition and on compensation.

3.2 Compensation

This assignment is well suited to group work in class: the extract can be divided into sections, with each group reporting their findings on the section assigned to them. We have found it useful to introduce group work early in the course, partly because it increases the element of enjoyment which is an important consideration in the course, and partly because students quickly realize that they can learn a lot from each other and boost each other's confidence. It is of course necessary to ensure that classroom layout enables 'buzz-groups' to work without interference from each other. It is for tutors to decide whether to circulate and join the buzz-groups, as participants or trouble-shooters; we have found it helpful and instructive to do so. Fun or no, it should be impressed on students that each group must formulate its findings coherently enough for them to be reported by a spokesperson as a useful contribution to class debate.

In this assignment, the focus of attention should be kept especially on compensation. The commentary on p. 22–25 is a sample of what might be expected of students. It may be reproduced and handed out after class discussion.

3.3 Cultural transposition; compensation

This assignment is actually best done (individually or in groups) by students at home; it can, however, be easily adapted to group work in class, particularly if each

Practical 3

group is instructed to go through the whole text, but to concentrate on translating only a designated section of it.

The text poses obvious problems of transposition, most of which concern remembering that the TT must be user-friendly for English-speaking immigrants in Spain: in particular, students should consider carefully whether certain phrases referring to specifically Spanish institutions should be translated at all, or whether they should be transferred verbatim with an English gloss given in brackets.

PRACTICAL 3

3.2 Compensation

COMMENTARY ON THE EXTRACT FROM *SEÑAS DE IDENTIDAD*

Before assessing the use of compensation in the TT, two strategic decisions need to be kept in mind: first, the ST observes a strictly contrived textual layout, reminiscent of the layout of free verse, a form which the translator has chosen to imitate closely; second, the multi-lingual and 'polyphonic' elements of the ST are interwoven with Goytisolo's critical message of political opposition to, and cultural alienation from, contemporary features of Spain. Both these considerations impose constraints on the TT, necessitating compromises and corresponding compensations. (Line numbers refer to the TT.)

line 2 Translating 'un cuadrado de césped' as 'a square of grass' represents an insufficient degree of cultural transposition in the TT: a less obtrusive and more culturally apt rendering would be 'a square lawn'.

line 3 The phrase 'a somber base held up...' is a multiple mistranslation: aptly transposed into English, the TT should read as 'raised on a modest but dignified plinth/pedestal stood...', a solution which involves not only amending 'sobrio' to 'sombrío' and substituting for 'base' the contextually more felicitous 'pedestal' (whose collocative connotation compensates, in context, for the fact that ST 'realzar' connotes a notion of 'holding up *proudly*'), but also a grammatical transposition of 'the... base held up the... statue' to the more idiomatic 'raised on a... pedestal stood the... statue' (compensation in kind).

line 4 As 'regalo de la Ciudad' cites the words written on the plinth, a plausible communicative translation should reflect the words that might be inscribed on a similar statue in English. Furthermore, for a British readership, 'the City' has far too specific cultural connotations which are inappropriate and distracting in the context. As a cultural transposition (and compensation in kind) we suggest: 'erected by the Municipality in honour of...'.

Practical 3

line 5   This line suffers significant translation loss in terms of the lack of idiomaticity occasioned, ironically, by altering the grammatical sequence of the ST. In this case, 'so said the plaque' would be a more contextually and culturally apt, and more clearly ironical, rendering than the grammatically transposed 'the plaque said so'.

line 6   The verbatim borrowing of 'Caudillo' into the TT introduces an element of exoticism which is likely to remain obscure in its reference for many English-speaking readers. In the ST, 'Caudillo Libertador' is, of course, a sarcastic expression alluding to Franco, but both the reference and the sarcasm are lost in the TT. A possible compensation (in kind), preserving both clarity of reference and an element of sarcasm, might be 'Liberator and Generalissimo'.

line 8   The image of a tightly-packed flock or herd of tourists being led, like dumb animals, towards the museum is lost in the TT; this loss could be compensated by editing the text to 'a press of tourists was flocking towards...' (compensation in place and in kind).

line 10   The translation loss involved in the referentially unclear phrase 'the card racks' could be easily compensated by the more explicit 'the racks displaying post-cards' (compensation by splitting).

line 11   The term 'Heráldica' is translated through compensation by splitting; however, the resulting phrase 'Heraldic Materials' is implausible and puzzling for the English reader. A better solution might be simply 'Heraldics'. Alternatively, one may argue that the TT requires a verbatim copying of the precise words reported in the ST. In this case, consistency requires the whole of 'Antigüedades Heráldica Soldados de Plomo' to be transposed as it stands into the TT. The objection to this solution is that, while the English-speaking reader can make sense of 'Antigüedades' and of 'Heráldica', 'Soldados de Plomo' will remain an incomprehensible exotic element.

line 14   The phrase 'ENTRANCE FREE' represents a discrepancy between British and American usage: the more common communicative equivalent in British usage is 'ADMISSION FREE'. However, it would be preferable in this context not to use either American or British idiom in an attempt at communicative translation, but to cite the ST formulation verbatim, since here again the ST is directly reporting the words displayed.

lines 17–18   The translation of 'SOUVENIR DE ESPAÑA' presents a problem of transposition. By the same reasoning as for the note on line 15, this caption should be transposed verbatim. This would cause no problems of comprehension; however, its logical knock-on effect would be to keep all the text from line 20 to line 32 also in its original ST form, which may be unacceptable for reasons of comprehension. The published TT has followed a solution whereby the entire text of the

Thinking Spanish Translation Teachers' Handbook

Spanish poster is rendered in English. A possible compromise might be to provide parallel Spanish and English texts of the caption:

SOUVENIR DE ESPAÑA   SOUVENIR OF SPAIN

line 27 It is unnecessary, and gratuitous, to transpose the ST caption 'HERE, YOUR NAME' to 'YOUR NAME. HERE ' in the TT.

line 32 The TT's 'quickly' seems to be an unnecessary addition: possibly this was intended as a compensation device used in the interests of idiomaticity, but its insertion seems rather gratuitous.

line 33 The rendering of 'curiosos' as 'curious people' is a necessary and successful piece of compensation by splitting. In the same line, the TT has lost (without trace or compensation) the ST's reference to '*dos* composiciones'. This could be easily remedied by editing the text to read '*two* photographic compositions', but this would entail further compensations in place: '*one* in which a bullfighter..., *the other* in which a Gypsy woman...'.

line 34 The literal rendering of 'con estampa de maestro' is not entirely successful in context: it seems to invite various non-metaphorical interpretations that are wholly inappropriate and distracting (for instance, 'with a stamp of the foot'). The suggested alternative, which retains the clichéd nature of the ST expression, is: 'with an air of mastery'.

line 35 The rendering 'Gypsy woman' is a successful and justifiable instance of compensation by splitting.

lines 35–36 The rendering 'very flashy she was' is a partially successful device used to compensate for the colloquial tone of the corresponding ST phrase. This compensation in kind would be more successful if the TT used the full colloquial idiom 'and very flashy she was, too'.

line 37 The rendering of 'endiablado' as 'devilish' is an unfortunate mistranslation: 'diabolical' might represent a reasonable compromise, but this still loses the ST's sense of 'bewitched or possessed'. One might compensate for this loss by for instance editing the TT to read as 'a diabolical torrent of broken Esperanto' (that is, by a mixture of compensation in place and compensation by splitting). In the same line, 'a characteristic example' is both unidiomatic and obscure: this should be edited (by communicative translation) as: 'a typical example/specimen'. A knock-on effect would be the need to edit the phrase 'a little Spaniard' to 'the little Spaniard'.

lines 37–38 The phrase 'Spaniard from the steppe' is an extraordinary piece of cultural transposition: in English-speaking cultures it is Russians, not Spaniards, who come from the steppes. Along with the proverbial rain, the Spaniard should probably come from 'the plain'; or, perhaps, 'the plains'. Line 38 contains a mistranslation of 'imagen trucada' as 'cut-off image', instead of 'trick photography'.

Practical 3

line 39 In the ST bits of French and English are mixed in with a mainly Spanish patter, whereas in the TT the patter is primarily in English with intermittent bits of Spanish and French. In order to compensate for this transposition, it would have been more appropriate to invert the order of the foreign phrases in the TT to read as 'messieurs et dames señoras y caballeros'. The same order of language mixing should be applied in lines 41–44, with the English phrases coming first in the list, followed by corresponding French and Spanish ones.

lines 40–41 The transposition of ST 'matadors and Gypsies' (which is meant to be an English phrase in the ST) to 'bullfighters and Gypsies' is both unnecessary and infelicitous: the point is that the ST uses the slightly more exotic borrowing from Spanish in preference to the anglicized 'bullfighters'. The phrase should be transposed verbatim into the TT. In the same lines, for no apparent reason, the TT has omitted the mixture of languages compounded by the ST.

lines 41–42 The ST contains correct French, which could easily have been transposed verbatim into the TT. It could be argued that, following on 'the ladies and gentlemen here present', a switch from second person address (your) to third person address (their) is necessary. However, for some incomprehensible reason, the translator has edited these phrases into *incorrect* French, for instance by altering 'vos pays' to 'leur pays' (even if the change from second person to third person were justified, the correct form is 'leurs pays'). A similar error occurs in line 42 where 'votre personnalité' has been rendered as mis-spelt 'leur personalité'. At the same time the incorrect French of ST 'affimer' has been corrected to 'affirmer' in the TT.

Lines 37–44 of the TT are of such poor quality as to deserve complete editing, perhaps to read as follows:

> in a diabolical torrent of broken Esperanto a typical specimen of the little Spaniard from the plains was explaining that this was a piece of trick photography with which the ladies and gentlemen messieurs et dames señoras y caballeros here present could surprise your friends and acquaintances dressed as matadors and gypsies toreadors et gitanes toreros y gitanas on your return to your respective countries vos pays d'origine a sus respectivos países and affirm your personality affirmer votre personnalité su personalidad with tales of your Spanish adventures aventures espagnoles aventuras españolas

Practical 4

NOTES FOR TUTORS

4.1 The formal properties of texts

This assignment is best done by students working individually, at home. The commentary accompanying our TT, on pp. 28–31 below, is more extensive than would be expected from students. In essence this commentary serves a pedagogic purpose as an example of the approach required. The TT and commentary may be reproduced for distribution to students at the end of the discussion in Practical 4.

4.2 The formal properties of texts; graphic

Guillermo de Torre's 'Paisaje plástico' provides the opportunity for a short discussion of the textual use of graphic form as a device that can be put to the service of textual meaning. As is obvious, the text, in this case a literary one, utilizes textual layout to trace out a schematic shape iconic of features of the objects named in the title (a landscape). While in a sense the example is an extreme case of graphic contrivance – and the use of such graphic devices is more peripheral in Western literature than that of phonic and prosodic patterns (in poetry, in particular) – there are two considerations that, in general, make graphic form worthy of the attention of translators. In the first place, the graphic layout of a text (even where it is less thematically salient than in Guillermo de Torre's text) always has a nuancing effect on the overall impact of a text. Second, the use of 'calligrams' is actually far more widespread in our culture than a consideration of literary genres might lead us to believe: it plays an important part in the design of advertisements, posters, greetings cards, Christmas cards and the like.

4.3 The formal properties of texts

This assignment is equally suitable for group work in class or at home. Apart from anything else, it is a useful stylistic exercise in verbal inventiveness (in general,

Practical 4

such exercises are an invaluable way of developing confidence, competence, and versatility *in the TL* – a too-often neglected aspect of translator training).

In completing and discussing this assignment, students should be directed to consider the extent to which the ST, for all that it is printed in prose form, has salient and patterned phonic/graphic and metric properties that give it a verse-like quality. They may, in fact, come to the conclusion that it is more like verse than prose.

The published TT on p. 32 may be reproduced for distribution in class after discussion of the student TTs and commentaries.

PRACTICAL 4

4.1 The formal properties of texts

COMMENTARY ON THE EXTRACT
FROM 'LA GOLONDRINA'

(i) Salient formal properties

The extract consists, both in terms of stanza layout, and in terms of metric properties, of two sections. The first four introductory lines are of variable length and, with the exception of the octosyllabic line 1, read metrically more like prose than verse. The opening two lines of the second stanza pick up a regular beat (8 syllables per line) which is interrupted by an irregular third line (14 syllables) followed by a line reverting to an octosyllabic pattern. From here on the metrical structure progresses, with the exception of lines 15 and 16, in sections of gradually shortening lines: two lines of 10 syllables are followed by two lines of 8 syllables and two lines of 7 syllables. Lines 15 and 16 revert to a length of 8 syllables, but are then followed by five short lines of 5 syllables each. A plausible metrical reading of the extract can be presented in outline form as follows:

   8; 14; 16; 12   11; 10; 14; 8; 12; 12; 8; 8; 7; 7; 8; 8; 5; 5; 5; 5; 5

The dynamics of these metric effects can be seen to have a function in relation to the theme: the progression of metric shortening serves to heighten the impression of an approaching object coming closer and closer, while the dips and changes in metric length evoke the dipping and zig-zagging flight of the swallow.

    From line 4 onwards ('gondoleando'), the extract is characterized by the suggestive use of carefully contrived neologisms with transparent meanings. These words are created in four different ways: 'gondoleando' is coined by converting the noun 'góndola' (itself phonically similar to 'golondrina') into a verb; 'lunala' is coined by compounding 'luna' and 'ala'; the pairs 'horitaña' – 'montazonte' and 'violondrina' – 'goloncelo' are coined by metathesis (inversion), that is, 'horizonte' and 'mon-taña' are roughly cut in half and the halves are interchanged, so

Practical 4

that they become 'horitaña' – 'montazonte'; the set of nonsense words 'golonfina... golonchilla' coined by a process of affixation, in which the word 'golondrina' is reduced to a stem 'golon-' and other words rhyming or assonating with '-drina' are affixed to this stem (for instance 'golon + fina'). These playful techniques of word coinage suggest vividly evocative metaphorical associations between the main thematic motif (the swallow) and a range of other objects (gondolas, musical instruments, exotic fruits, and so on).

(ii) TT

> There isn't a moment[1] to lose
> Here comes the monoseasonal[2] swallow
> Bringing antipodean accents ever closer and closer[3]
> The swallow comes swallowgliding[4]
>
> To the horountain from the mountizon[5]   5
> The violinswallow and the swallocello[6]

1   The choice of 'there isn't a moment' over the more literal 'there is no time' serves to reinforce the sense of urgency in the text.
2   The option of 'monotemporal' is rejected for several reasons: it is too literal, too formal in register, and less phonically satisfying than 'monoseasonal' which contains a phonic echo of the initial [s] of 'swallow'.
3   The alliteration of 'antipodean accents' partially renders the ST alliteration of 'acento antípoda...acercan'. Tension is heightened by the phrase 'closer and closer', which, aside from suitably lengthening the line, also allows for a third alliterating element 'and' to complete the series.
4   This solution represents a compromise: while the idea of a smooth, gliding motion is retained, the ST's explicit image of a gondola is sacrificed for the sake of a phonic effect imitating the partial phonic similarity of 'gondoleando' and 'golondrina' through the repetition of 'swallow'. Though the option exists of coining a verb 'gondoliering' for the TT, the point of this is vitiated by the fact that this neologism bears no phonetic similarity to the word 'swallow'.
5   The TT imitates the method by which the ST neologisms have been coined: that is, it roughly permutes the halves of 'hor-izon' and 'mount-ain' .
6   Here the TT is unable exactly to imitate the principle by which the ST neologisms were coined: that is, by transposition of the elements of 'violin-cello' and 'swal-low' (which would yield the connotatively and phonically unsatisfactory 'violinlow' and 'swalcello'). We have chosen instead to retain the metaphors of musical instruments by combining 'violin' and 'cello' with the forms 'swallow' and 'swallo'.

>   Swallooping[7] down this very dawn from the moonwing[8]
>   At full speed it's arriving
>   Here here comes the swallowswift[9]
>   Here here comes the swallowgift   10
>   Here comes the swallowlift
>   Here comes the swallowdrift[10]
>   Comes the swallowchime
>   Comes the swallowclime
>   Here comes the swallowrhyme   15
>   Here comes the swallowthyme[11]
>   The swallowbine[12]

7   The option of this extra play on words is taken up by way of compensation of the slight loss of playful phonic effects in the previous line (compensation in kind and place): 'swallooping' is a portmanteau coinage combining 'swallow' and 'swooping'.

8   The compound 'moonwing' is coined by simple imitation of the ST coinage 'luna' (moon) + 'ala' (wing).

9   The coinage 'swallowswift', besides being a playful coinage trading on the meanings of 'swift' (bird) and 'swift' (fast), allows for convenient rhymes to be found for the following three lines. Its connotation compensates for connotations of speed and allegresse conveyed at other points in the ST, but the main reason for choosing it is phonic.

10 The rhyming compound coinages in these lines represent an extremely free rendering of the ST. Besides the important phonic effects these rhyming words maintain in the TT, the main consideration for their choice is one of connotative effect: they all suggest positive attitudes to the swallow and both 'lift' and 'drift' suggest a light, airy movement which is thematically appropriate.

11 The ST contains a single series of full rhymes and assonances running through lines 9–21. Such a single series would have been extremely difficult to construct in the TT, and would, in any case, tend to be counter-productive: the effect might well be to trivialise the TT. In our TT we have compromised by using a rhyme scheme AAAA—BBBB—CCB—DD which more or less parallels the dips and changes in metric length (see the comments about formal properties of the ST above). In short, the rhyme-scheme, running tandem with metric length, serves (through compensation in kind) to highlight the thematic motif of the swallow's flight in the TT, just as it does in the ST. Literal meaning has been substantially sacrificed to achieving appropriate phonic effects.

12 This coinage is an extremely free rendering of the corresponding ST word. The word 'swallowbine' is coined rather like ST 'goloncello', combining 'swallow' with part of 'Columbine'. Through the associations of 'Columbine' the TT attempts to convey something of the connotation of affection implicit in the ST 'niña', but the main reason for this choice is phonic.

Practical 4

    The swallowfine
    The swallowcline
    The swallowbreeze   20
    The swallowtease.[13]

13 In metric terms the TT attempts to reproduce something of the relative proportions of the ST, though it does so in terms of stressed syllables per line, rather than a simple syllable count. In fact, the TT is in the form of strong stress metre, with longer lines having a greater, and shorter lines a smaller, number of stressed syllables.

PRACTICAL 4

4.3 The formal properties of texts

                PUBLISHED TT OF 'TOCO TU BOCA...'

Target text

7

I TOUCH your mouth, I touch the edge of your mouth with my finger, I am drawing it as if it were something my hand was sketching, as if for the first time your mouth opened a little, and all I have to do is close my eyes to erase it and start all over again, every time I can make the mouth I want appear, the mouth which my hand chooses and sketches on your face, and which by some chance   5 that I do not seek to understand coincides exactly with your mouth which smiles beneath the one my hand is sketching on you.

    You look at me, from close up you look at me, closer and closer and then we play cyclops, we look closer and closer at one another and our eyes get larger, they come closer, they merge into one and the two cyclopses look at each other,   10 blending as they breathe, our mouths touch and struggle in gentle warmth, biting each other with their lips, barely holding their tongues on their teeth, playing in corners where a heavy air comes and goes with an old perfume and a silence. Then my hands go to sink into your hair, to cherish slowly the depth of your hair while we kiss as if our mouths were filled with flowers or with fish, with lively   15 movements and dark fragrance. And if we bite each other the pain is sweet, and if we smother each other in a brief and terrible sucking in together of our breaths, that momentary death is beautiful. And there is but one saliva and one flavor of ripe fruit, and I feel you tremble against me like a moon on the water.

                Reprinted from Julio Cortázar, *Hopscotch*, translated by
Gregory Rabassa (New York, Pantheon Books, 1966, p. 33), copyright © 1966 by
                                      Random House, Inc.

Practical 5

NOTES FOR TUTORS

5.1 The formal properties of texts

This assignment is intended to be done in class, but it can equally well be done at home. The commentary on pp. 36–37 may be reproduced for distribution to students at the end of class discussion of the text. The handout itself may generate lively discussion, if time allows.

The assignment illustrates the need for translators to be aware of the nature of lexical items in a ST (not just of their meanings and their register, but also of their historical origins) and of the thematically and textually crucial function they may play in certain kinds of text. The ST, the theme it develops, and the central irony on which Goytisolo's argument rests, are crucially dependent on the textual deployment of a word-system (as defined on p. 67 of the coursebook) consisting of *Spanish words with evidently Arabic origins*. In completing the assignment, students should be guided to reconstruct this word-system in the ST by highlighting Arabic loan-words in the ST. (We provide a list in our commentary on p. 37.)

5.2 The formal properties of texts

This assignment is intended to be started in class, and completed at home, either in groups or individually. If some of the work is done in groups, it is vital to ensure that each group looks at the entire extract. If time allows, a lively discussion can be generated by asking students to evaluate the success of the TT given on pp. 40–43.

The assignment makes especially clear the need for an initial thematic and stylistic analysis before strategic decisions, for instance relating to syntax, can be taken. We are not suggesting that students should be expected to provide an exhaustive analysis, but simply that they do the same kind of preliminary work as is necessary in preparing a textual analysis. The Martín-Santos text also shows very clearly the need for due attention to contextual information, including the immediate context of the actual passage itself. Taking the contextual information into

Practical 5

account brings out especially sharply the fact that apparently opaque details in the ST can be resolved by a more holistic view of the text. Comparing our TT with student TTs should make for an interesting, lively and valuable session.

Students should, in particular, be guided towards considering the function of the cluttered, uninterrupted syntax in the ST: for instance, its contribution to the disorienting, 'kaleidoscopic', shifting perspectives of the description, and the mood of the text as a whole. A major strategic question to ask is whether, and to what extent, these functions can be adequately fulfilled in a translation that breaks the text into small, self-contained sentences punctuated by full stops.

PRACTICAL 5

5.1 The formal properties of texts

COMMENTARY ON THE EXTRACT FROM
REIVINDICACIÓN DEL CONDE DON JULIÁN

Strategic problems

For appreciating the thematic point of the ST, it is important to note the word system of Spanish words with Arabic origins distributed throughout the text. Goytisolo's main point consists in the implicit irony or paradox of a Spanish cultural purism that looks down upon Arab cultures while making extensive use of a vocabulary of terms and notions for which Spanish is indebted to Arabic.

The principal strategic problem of translation lies in the fact that the English language does not contain a sufficient stock of words borrowed from Arabic, and that the relationship between Anglo-Saxon and Arab cultures does not in any way replicate the indebtedness of Spanish to Arabic. Thus, the irony of the ST is extremely hard to reproduce in an English TT based on a word system of Arabic loan-words. Cultural transplantation, with Latin (and Greco- Roman), or for that matter French, culture taking the place occupied by Arabic in the ST, would be feasible; but it is counterindicated by the fact that Anglo-Saxon cultural purists cannot plausibly be portrayed as looking down on their Greco- Roman, or Norman French, heritage: both Latin and French have a definite snob value in Anglo-Saxon cultures, which Arabic does not command in Hispanic cultures. To this must be added the fact that the theme of Goytisolo's text is specific to the relationship between Spanish and Arabic. Thus, cultural transplantation would, it seems, doubly vitiate the purpose of the TT.

This leaves the translator with either the rather difficult option of compiling lists of Arabic loan-words in English, and trying to weave them into a plausible TT whose irony is directed, as in the ST, at Spanish cultural purism; or resorting to a TT that retains the Spanish/Arabic words verbatim, and constructs a textual exegesis round them.

Practical 5

The word system of Arabic loan-words in the ST is as follows:

algodón, algarrobo, alfalfa, aljibes, albercas, almacenes, dársenas, alquerías, alcobas, alacenas, zaguanes, sofás, alfombras, jarros, almohadas, aldeas, ajuar, alhajas, fulana, alcurnia, ajedrez, alquitrán, alborozos, juergas, zalemas, albricias, carcajadas, arroz, aceitunas, alubias, berenjenas, zanahorias, adobo, azafrán, alcachofa, aderezada, espinaca, albóndigas, aceite, caramelo, azúcar, jarabe, sorbete.

PRACTICAL 5

5.2 The formal properties of texts

COMMENTARY ON THE EXTRACT FROM
TIEMPO DE SILENCIO

(i) Salient formal properties

The most salient strategic properties presented by this ST concern its complex syntactic organisation. The extract is made up of a series of co-ordinated (paratactic) syntactic units, each with its internal hypotactic and/or paratactic elaboration, and each presenting one of a series of juxtaposed images, functioning as metaphors representing the protagonist's impressions and sensations. (It is, of course, essential to remember the vital contextual information that these impressions and sensations refer to a drunken visit to a brothel.) Some of the co-ordinated syntactic units differ from the rest in that they have no explicit nominal head (they consist, in their turn, of co-ordinated adjectival constituents directly qualifying the room described, but not explicitly mentioned, in the ST); other co-ordinated syntactic units can each be identified as headed by a nominal nucleus: 'capitoné', 'lugar', 'túnel', 'laguna', 'cabina', 'cabin-log', 'camarote', 'barquilla', 'ascensor', 'calabozo', 'cesto de inmundicia', 'calabozo', 'aniquilación inversa', 'sala'. The series of co-ordinated units reveals a dynamic pattern in terms of relative length: starting with a long first syntactic unit, they gradually decrease in size until we reach the shortest unit ('laguna estigia'). This is followed again by a long, complex syntactic unit and a series of units of decreasing length terminating in the short 'barquilla hecha de mimbres que montgolfiera', after which the syntactic units gradually increase in length again. The pattern is not exactly symmetrical – the ante-penultimate and the last unit are the longest and syntactically most complex, with a slightly shorter unit sandwiched between them – but it has a thematically important effect in reinforcing the sensation of an alternately focused and receding image.

Since the syntactic patterning of the ST is distinctive, and since the 'kaleidoscopic' and 'dizzying' impact of the text (including clear thematic suggestions of nausea) is at least in part mediated by the syntax – Martín-Santos is noted for his

38

use of syntax to parallel and underline thematic motifs – a major strategic consideration for the translator must be to ensure that, in the TT too, syntactic patterning is used to reinforce textual content. This can probably best be achieved by attempting to recreate in the TT the construction of a single sentence which replicates the ST's juxtaposition of sixteen co-ordinated syntactic units of appropriate lengths. That is to say, the translator should attempt to reflect as much of the syntactic dynamics of the ST as possible.

Another salient, and thematically significant, property of the ST is its use of overlapping word systems. We can distinguish at least eight overlapping word systems in the ST:

1 a word system of technical, scientific words (thematically relevant in the light of contextual information about the protagonist who is a medical researcher) – for instance, 'fosforescente', 'fibrosa-táctil', 'experimento', 'giroscópica', 'placenta', 'meconio';
2 a word system of terms associated with childbirth and maternity (with obvious thematic relevance to the plot) – for instance, 'materna', 'briza', 'amamanta', 'cuna', 'placenta', 'meconio', 'deciduas', 'matriz', 'oviducto', 'ovario';
3 a word system of references to women (thematically relevant in the context of a brothel, though often in ironic ways) – for instance, 'materna', 'prostituta', 'patrona', 'sirena', 'mujer', 'puta';
4 a word system of 'architectural' features – including 'túnel', 'cabin-log', 'calabozo', 'ascensor', 'sala de retirada, 'sala de visitas', 'sala para los detritus';
5 a word system of references to modes of travel introduced by 'una travesía secreta' – including 'vagon-lit', 'camarote', 'barquilla', 'ascensor';
6 a word system of terms associated with the sea – including 'laguna', 'tifones', 'mar', 'sirena', 'pez', 'encallan';
7 a word system with exotic, multi-cultural referents (these words add to the disorienting, kaleidoscopic quality of the text) – for instance, 'vagon-lit', 'bordelesas', 'cabin-log', 'faruest', 'índico', 'cormoran';
8 a word system of hyphenated coinages, some of them oxymoronic (such coinages are typical of Martín-Santos's writing in general) – for instance, 'oscura-luminosa', 'fibrosa-táctil', 'gusano-cuerpo'.

Both for an initial comprehension of the ST, and for the construction of an effective TT, the distribution of these word systems throughout the text, and their cumulative impact, constitute important strategic considerations for the translator.

Thinking Spanish Translation Teachers' Handbook

(ii) TT with comments on points of detail

Spheroidal, phosphorescent, booming, obscure-luminous, fibro-tactile, gathered in pleats, caressing, soothing, paralysingly covered in protective folds,[1] heavily scented,[2] maternal, impregnated with alcohol dribbled[3] from the mouth, bluish quilt sometimes gilded by an anaemic lightbulb whose brightness hurts nocturnal[4] eyes, soporific, commanding a quiet murmur,[5] degrading, the prostitute's cup of scorn for the drunkard, place where the madam[6] becomes father confessor laying down clear and correct[7] rules prescribing how to avoid sins of the flesh, longitudinal, tunnel welling with nausea, earth-coloured as the worm-body comes into contact with the mass that imprisons-surrounds it,[8] lacking in

1. The ST uses a selection of rather oblique and bizarre epithets to highlight a perception of the brothel. Up to this point the TT can afford to be quite closely modelled on the idiosyncrasies of the ST, including the calqued coinages 'obscure-luminous' and 'fibro-tactile'.
2. The choice of the more explicit 'heavily scented', in preference over such options as 'odorous', 'pungent', 'smelly', and so on, is motivated by contextual considerations: the atmosphere of a brothel is likely to be over-scented with heavy perfume.
3. A more literal rendering would be 'spilt'; however, the choice of 'dribbled' is more contextually and collocatively plausible in its connotation of drunken helplessness.
4. This solution rejects the more literal 'noctambulant' as idiomatically implausible. The choice of 'nocturnal' retains an associative link with zoological terminology (see the comments on a word system of scientific terms). The ST's connotations of 'sleepwalking' have been lost in the TT: the effort of compensating for these minor losses would be counter-productive.
5. This is a non-literal, communicative rendering; 'suitable only for murmuring' would certainly be unidiomatic to the point of incomprehensibility. The ST's notion that this is a place where one would feel one had to speak in hushed tones is more idiomatically rendered by a communicative circumlocution.
6. This is more explicit than ST 'patrona', but 'madam' is the culturally, contextually and idiomatically correct choice.
7. The appropriate rendering of the cliché 'rectas normas' is problematic here. Literal translation is inappropriate, but there is also a lack of a suitable communicative rendering. Our choice was influenced by indirect reference to the notion of 'rules of correct behaviour'.
8. As remarked in note 1, the ST frequently uses oblique and bizarre metaphors. The safest resort in translating these is to seek a compromise between a fairly close calquing of the ST (for instance, 'worm-body' and 'imprisons-surrounds') and a reasonable degree of TL idiomaticity, achieved through grammatical transposition (for instance, 'comes into contact with'). It is not implausible to regard the ST metaphor as an oblique description of sexual intercourse, but it would be a serious translation loss to make this bluntly or crudely obvious in the TT.

Practical 5

gravitational force like an experiment not yet completed, gyroscopic, oriented towards a north,[9] chosen for a furtive crossing, Stygian lagoon, furnished with a metallic bunk from which the outstretched and languid body falls to a barely lower softness,[10] wagon-lit[11] compartment travelling at a hundred and thirty kilometers per hour across the Bordeaux plains,[12] Wild West log-cabin[13] where not a scalp remains, cabin heaving in an Indian Ocean[14] storm when not even the yellow cormorant[15] can fly in the typhoons, wicker basket of a balloon montgolfiering[16] along, elevator hurtling towards the top of a skyscraper of stretched rubber, immobile prison cell where man's solitude is proven, basket

9   The ST creates an unusual metaphor, thematically linked both with the word system of scientific terms made particularly relevant by the protagonist's medical background and with the word system of references to travel. The safest solution for rendering this metaphor is, as in earlier cases, to aim at a compromise between faithful calquing of the ST (as for instance 'gyroscopic') and TL idiomaticity (as for instance 'an experiment not yet completed').

10 Similar considerations apply as in notes 8 and 9. The choice of 'bunk' rather than 'bench' or 'work bench' is motivated partly by the immediately following reference to 'wagon-lit', and partly by the fact – anticipated in line 18 of the ST – that the protagonist will later be held in police custody.

11 The textual effect of the spelling 'wagon-lit' is to mitigate the exoticism of this loan-word by the use of a Spanish transliteration. In our TT we have reverted to the orthographic form 'wagon-lit', this being the normal form in which the term has been assimilated into English.

12 The phrase 'landas bordelesas' presents a problem of comprehension. Presumably this is simply one of a number of references to journeys in exotic places.

13 One of a series of references to faraway places, 'faruest' is a transliteration of English 'Far West' (compare 'vagon-lit'). The de-exoticising effect of the orthographic adaptation is better conveyed in the TT by the clichéd 'Wild West', whose romantic associations also seem contextually apt. The inversion of 'log-cabin' to 'cabin-log' may serve the same de-exoticising purpose as the transliteration of 'faruest' in the ST; to retain this inversion in the TT would lead to a marked case of exoticism bordering on potential incomprehension.

14 The TT solution represents a case of compensation by splitting; however, this is a literally exact rendering of 'índico' (East Indian).

15 The ST reference to 'amarillo cormorán', while clearly exotic and evocative of an ornithological designation, is somewhat obscure. The fairly anodyne rendering 'yellow cormorant' retains these features to a degree.

16 The ST's transparent principle of coinage, creating a verb by allusion to the balloonist Montgolfier brothers, can be plausibly applied in English to produce the neologism 'montgolfiering', whose intended meaning is made transparent by the particularizing phrase 'of a balloon'.

Thinking Spanish Translation Teachers' Handbook

of ordure, sediment in which, reduced to excrement,[17] the occupant awaits the arrival of the black waters that will flush[18] him seaward past grey rats and past sewers, prison cell once again in which the figure of a mermaid with an astounding female-fish-tail is slowly and laboriously scratched out on the flaking whitewashed wall with a nail,[19] guarded by the large figure of a woman who cradles her, caressed by the soft figure of a woman who suckles,[20] crib, placenta, meconium, afterbirth, womb, oviduct, pure empty ovary, inverse annihilation in which the ovum in an antiprotonic universe is split into its two

17   In terms of register, the lexical items 'ordure', 'sediment' and 'excrement' are apt to form part of a word system of scientific terms created in the TT in imitation of the ST. A less elevated or more vulgar choice of terms would falsify the inexplicit nature of the ST.
18   By the choice of 'flush', with its fairly explicit lavatory connotations, the TT risks being less subtle and indirect than the ST. However, the TT remains far from crude in its reinforcement of a metaphor that is implicit in the ST.
19   The need for a syntactically smooth, comprehensible and idiomatic TT rendering dictates a substantial reorganisation of the sequence in which phrases are presented in the ST. It is on this basis that we reject the syntactically more closely calqued, but cumbersome and practically incomprehensible, 'where with a nail slowly is being drawn laboriously by scratching on the whitewashed wall the figure of a mermaid...'.
20   It is tempting to mark the syntactic break between 'suckles' and 'cradle' by a semi-colon as opposed to a mere comma: however, since the ST refrains from such a clear signalling of syntactic breaks, preferring to put the onus for their recognition on the reader, it is preferable to do the same in the TT. In any case, the syntactic break is marked by the fact that 'cradle' opens a long paratactic series of nominals (six nouns and a noun phrase).

Practical 5

former components and Matias has unbegun not to exist,[21] this is the retiring room, visitors' lounge, lumber-room,[22] the room for drunkards from good families who arrive one drowned night and run aground[23] on the only whore who has not been able to work and who looks at them uncomprehendingly while they lie amid the orange peel and potato peelings[24] and are reconciled and redeemed.[25]

21   The ST's construction of a paradoxical, oxymoronic phrase requires an idiomatic reconstruction. In a literal translation calqued on the ST, the paradoxicality of the phrase would probably be ascribed to translationese, rather than to a deliberate oxymoronic effect in the text.

22   While 'lumber-room' is not a close literal rendering of 'sala para los detritus', a less idiomatic, more elaborate, and more closely calqued phrase would break the continuity with the idiomatic clichés 'retiring room' and 'visitors' lounge'. The compound word 'lumber-room' is a semantically apt cliché to add to the list.

23   The ST figure of speech can be fairly literally rendered without loss of idiomaticity. The two main contenders for rendering 'encallan' are 'run aground' and 'are shipwrecked' — the latter of the two is more strongly and openly marked for its textual echoes of the seafaring motif running through the text; we prefer the more subtle and less blatant 'run aground'.

24   For the English-speaking reader the juxtaposition of orange peel and potato peelings may seem culturally odd, though this is certainly not the case for the Spanish reader of the ST. The safest solution is to translate the ST phrase fairly literally, allowing for the cultural oddity this lends to the TT, but without creating a further oddity by making the TT linguistically unidiomatic. In order to maintain idiomaticity in the TT, the force of ST 'revueltos' (inexactly rendered by 'lie') has been sacrificed.

25   A possible literal rendering of 'salvan' is 'saved'. Our preference for 'redeemed' is due to the extra emphasis this word lends to the religious connotations in the text (see elsewhere in the extract 'father confessor', 'sins of the flesh'). These connotations, as well as the 'punchline' effect of the final clause, are further highlighted by the alliteration in '**r**econciled and **r**edeemed', which compensates for other alliterations in this section of the ST (for instance, 'con **m**irada incomprensiva los **m**ira **m**ientras que...').

Practical 6

NOTES FOR TUTORS

6.1 The formal properties of texts; discourse and intertextuality

This assignment is best carried out at home, but can still be done by students working in groups. The commentary and TT on pp. 46–47 may be reproduced and given to students, before or after class discussion, at the tutor's discretion.

A useful way to start the assignment is by suggesting that, after having carefully read through the extract, students systematically highlight the rhetorical devices and the cohesion marking elements in the ST. This will also present an opportunity, for each of the highlighted details, to invite students to offer alternative ways in which the textual effects of the ST's discourse level features could be rendered in an English TT; including, of course, raising the vital question of whether each and every one of these features should be rendered in the TT.

6.2 Speed translation

This assignment works equally well when done by students individually or in groups; in either case, time should be given, if at all possible, to comparing the TTs produced. The ST for the assignment is given on p. 49 below.

PRACTICAL 6

6.1 The formal properties of texts; discourse and intertextuality

COMMENTARY ON THE EXTRACT FROM
DEL SENTIMIENTO TRÁGICO DE LA VIDA

(i) Strategic considerations

On the sentential and discourse levels, the salient formal properties of the extract are twofold: first, the varied rhetorical devices (for instance, the alternation of interrogative, indicative and imperative sentential forms) that mediate the extract's character as a mixture between soliloquy and direct personal address to the reader; second, the various cohesion-marking units and devices that play a vitally important role in mediating the argument put forward by the author, and the *cogency* of this argument.

In the first instance, a full and correct appreciation of the role of the ST's rhetorical patterns, as well as of the cohesion markers that signpost its thematic development, is an essential precondition for understanding the ideas developed in the extract, and the way they hang together. In the second place, a major strategic decision for the translator of the extract is whether and how to accommodate these rhetorical patterns and cohesion markers in a TT; a TT that failed to take full account of them would run the risk of not doing justice to the logically tight structure of the ST, while, on the other hand, a TT excessively marked by rhetorical conceits and redundant cohesion markers may easily become too patronizing, heavy-handed and smacking of translationese. A difficult balance needs to be found for maintaining, but not over-marking, the coherent flow of ideas through the TT.

Practical 6

(ii)   TT

A disease? Perhaps; but he who pays no heed to his disease is heedless of his health, and man is an animal essentially and substantially diseased. A disease? Perhaps it may be, like life itself to which it is thrall, and perhaps the only health possible may be death; but this disease is the fount of all vigorous health. From the depth of this anguish, from the abyss of the feeling of our mortality, we   5
emerge into the light of another heaven, as from the depth of Hell Dante emerged to behold the stars once again –

e quindi uscimmo a riveder le stelle.

Although this meditation upon mortality may soon induce in us a sense of anguish, it fortifies us in the end. Retire, reader, into yourself and imagine a slow   10
dissolution of yourself – the light dimming about you – all things becoming dumb and soundless, enveloping you in silence – the objects that you handle crumbling away between your hands – the ground slipping from under your feet – your very memory vanishing as if in a swoon – everything melting away from you into nothingness and you yourself also melting away – the very conscious-   15
ness of nothingness, merely as the phantom harbourage of a shadow, not even remaining to you.

I have heard it related of a poor harvester who died in a hospital bed, that when the priest went to anoint his hands with the oil of extreme unction, he refused to open his right hand, which clutched a few dirty coins, not considering   20
that very soon neither his hand nor he himself would be his own any more. And so we close and clench, not our hand, but our heart, seeking to clutch the world in it.

Reprinted from Miguel de Unamuno, *The Tragic Sense of Life*, translated by Amalia Elguera (London: Macmillan; Collins: Fontana Library, 1962, pp. 57–8), © Herederos de Miguel de Unamuno and © Macmillan, 1921.

PRACTICAL 6

6.2. Speed translation

Assignment

In a time limit set by your tutor, produce a stylistically appropriate translation of the following ST, paying due attention to layout.

Contextual information

The text is a poster advertising an academic conference.

Practical 6

Marzo '92
I CONGRESO ANGLO-HISPANO

MARTES, 24
19,30 APERTURA Y PLENARIA
de *J. H. Elliott.*
(Foro Iberoamericano, La Rábida).

MIERCOLES, 25
Sesiones de la mañana 1
MENTALIDADES.
LAS LENGUAS HISPÁNICAS EN LA ÉPOCA DE COLON.
LIBROS DE VIAJES Y CRÓNICAS DEL NUEVO MUNDO, S. XIV-XVI.
18,00 PLENARIA de *E. Martinell.*
(Foro Iberoamericano, La Rábida).

JUEVES, 26
Sesiones de la mañana 2
MESIANISMO.
NEBRIJA Y LA TRADICIÓN GRAMATICAL HISPÁNICA.
LITERATURA DE CONVERSOS Y MORISCOS; ESCRITORAS DE LOS S. XV-XVII.
19,00 PLENARIA de *M. Frenk.* Recepción.
(Ayuntamiento de Moguer).

VIERNES, 27
Sesiones de la mañana 3
GRUPOS DE PODER, 1.
LAS LENGUAS HISPÁNICAS EN SU VARIEDAD SOCIAL.
LITERATURA HISPANO-AMERICANA DE LA ÉPOCA COLONIAL.

19,00 PLENARIA de *C. H. Griffin.*
(Riotinto).

SABADO, 28
Sesiones de la mañana 4
GRUPOS DE PODER, 2.
LAS LENGUAS HISPÁNICAS EN SU DESARROLLO HISTÓRICO, 1.
ENCUENTRO DE CULTURAS COMO TEMA LITERARIO, 1.
18,00 PLENARIA de *P. E. Russell.*
(La Rábida) Homenaje a G. Ribbans.

LUNES, 30
Sesiones de la mañana,
MARGINADOS, 1.
LAS LENGUAS HISPÁNICAS EN SU DESARROLLO HISTÓRICO, 2.
ENCUENTRO DE DOS CULTURAS COMO TEMA LITERARIO, 2.
19,30 PLENARIA de *J. M. Lepe Blanch.*
Recepción.
(Ayuntamiento de Palos).

MARTES, 31
Sesiones de la mañana, 6.
MARGINADOS, 2
LA LENGUA ESPAÑOLA EN SU VARIEDAD GEOGRÁFICA.
RAÍCES EUROPEAS DE LA
LITERATURA
HISPANOAMERICANA.
19,00 PLENARIA de *F. Morán* y Clausura.
(Gran Teatro, Huelva).

―――――

(Las sesiones de la mañana se celebrarán en la casa Colón de Huelva de 9,00 a 1,30. Cada sesión consistirá en cuatro ponencias, con un descanso de 10,30 a 11,00 y terminará con una mesa redonda a las 12,30 h.)

HUELVA '92
PATRONATO PROVINCIAL QUINTO CENTENARIO

Practical 7

NOTES FOR TUTORS

7.1 Particularizing, generalizing and partially overlapping translation

This assignment is best done working individually, but it can equally well be done in groups, whether in class or at home. If it is done in groups in class, allocating a section of the text to each group for close scrutiny is a good way of ensuring that the whole text can be covered in subsequent plenary discussion. The suggested analysis on pp. 52–55 may be reproduced for distribution to students, preferably at the end of the discussion.

In this assignment, students are asked to carry out a somewhat artificial task, concentrating on one single issue: literal meaning. It is advisable to explain at the outset that, of course, translating can never be such a single-minded activity: the purpose of this assignment is to use an artificially intensive exercise in order to sharpen students' understanding of how widespread particularizing, generalizing and partially overlapping translation are, and how multifarious their operation is. Hence the detailed analysis given here. Mastering a technique for recognizing these features makes it much easier both to identify and to solve the problems raised by literal meaning in any given text. However, students' attention should be drawn to the note at the end of our analysis. The aim of the course is not to build up ever more exhaustive techniques of linguistic or textual analysis (which a working translator would not have the time to apply); on the contrary, in assessing a TT, literal exactitude is only one of many aspects to be evaluated, and the test of literal meaning would only be applied to salient points isolated as problematic in this respect.

7.2 Speed translation

The text given here on pp. 56–57 may be reproduced and handed out for speed translation (not gist translation) in class. It is 402 words long. It would be reasonable to allow 20 minutes for the first two paragraphs and 25 minutes for the whole text. Discussing the translation in class will need at least another 15 minutes.

PRACTICAL 7

7.1 Particularizing, generalizing and partially overlapping translation

DEGREES OF APPROXIMATION IN LITERAL MEANING IN THE EXTRACT FROM *THE LIFE OF SAINT TERESA OF AVILA*

ST 6–7 Era mi padre... hijos.

1. 'fond of reading' is a partially overlapping translation of 'aficionado a leer': the TT loses the strong sense of 'keen enthusiast' conveyed by 'aficionado', and substitutes for it a weak notion of mere 'fondness'.
2. 'holy books' is a misleading partial translation of 'buenos libros' ; the TT adds the notion that the books referred to are biblical, or at the very least, devotional, and excludes the possibility that some of them may be edifying secular works. (The false impression created in the TT is of a reader with rather narrow, pious tastes.)
3. 'in Spanish' is a plausible particularization of 'de romance' (implying contrast with 'in Latin'); nevertheless the generalization 'in the vernacular' (which retains this contrast) would be a safer, less contentious and yet fully adequate alternative in the overall textual and historical context of the ST.
4. partial translation results from misplacing 'too' in the TT: the notion of 'books in the vernacular *as well as* in Latin' implied by the ST ('ansí... de romance', *not* 'ansí sus hijos') has been mistakenly replaced in the TT by the idea of 'his children *as well as* he himself'.

Ed. TT: My father was an avid reader of good books, and even had some in the vernacular so that his children might read them.

ST 7–10 Éstos... siete años.

1. 'pains' is a partially overlapping translation of 'cuidado'; while it keeps the notion of 'effort', the sense of solicitude is lost from the TT, to be replaced by a notion of 'uphill work'.

Practical 7

2 'teaching us' is a mistranslation of 'hacernos' ('making us ...', 'causing us to ...'): the TT omits the element of discipline in making sure that prayers are said regularly.
3 'educating us' is an unduly narrow particularization of 'ponernos'; while focusing attention on the element of 'instruction' (clearly not the only factor at issue in the ST), it excludes the notion of 'teaching by example'.
4 'certain Saints' is a partial translation of 'algunos Santos': the notion of plurality is common to the ST and the TT; but the ST's suggestion of an eclectic choice is replaced by a suggestion of exclusivity (only *some* Saints, but *not* others) in the TT. This misconstrual, small in itself, has a distorting effect on Saint Teresa's description of her parents. This is the second suggestion we have seen of a narrow-minded piety attributed to them in the TT extract, without justification from the ST: the cumulative effect is a serious misrepresentation of the ST.
5 As discussed in the sample analysis given in the coursebook (p. 94), 'rouse' is a particularization of 'despertar' ('wake/awaken/stir up/arouse'), introducing an element of intensity to the TT which is not present in the ST; because of its collocative echoes of 'spiritual awakening', we prefer 'awaken', although 'open my eyes' offers an attractive alternative.

Ed. TT: These, along with the care my mother took to make us say our prayers and to instil in us a devotion to Our Lady and to various Saints, began to awaken me at the age, I suppose, of six or seven.

ST 10–11 Ayudábame... muchas.

1 'never saw' is an idiomatic particularization of 'no ver' (literally, but less effectively, rendered as 'did not see'), but it possibly contributes still further to the excessive piety introduced in the TT.
2 'inclined', while constituting a case of justifiable grammatical transposition of a Spanish nominal into an English verbal adjective, represents another instance of partial translation: the TT makes explicit reference to virtuous *proclivitie*s implicit in the ST, but omits the ST's explicit reference to virtuous *behaviour*. (Once again the notion of 'teaching by example' has been omitted from the TT; see ST 7–10 note 3.) It is both possible and preferable to avoid restricting the literal meaning of the TT to either *proclivities* or *behaviour*; this can be achieved simply by omitting 'inclined to'.
3 'and many virtues they had' is a particularizing translation of 'Tenían muchas', motivated by an attempt at idiomatic translation. It is possible, and preferable, to avoid a repetition of 'virtue' in the TT.

Ed. TT: It was a help to me that I saw nothing other than virtues in my parents; and they had many of these.

ST 11–15 Era mi padre... de piadad.

1. 'most charitable' is a particularizing translation of 'de mucha caridad', because the words 'charity' and 'charitable' in modern English denote only a part of the set of qualities denoted by Teresa's term 'caridad' (= theological 'caritas'). To come closer to the full meaning of 'caridad', it may be necessary to add 'devout' to 'charity' (an example of compensation by splitting).
2. 'be persuaded' is a particularizing translation of 'se pudo acabar'; the TT retains the idea of 'coming to terms with', but it has gratuitously added the notion of some external agent of persuasion. If we take 'se pudo acabar' as a reflexive, rather than an impersonal, construction, 'be persuaded' amounts to a mistranslation.
3. 'pity' is a particularization of 'piadad' that highlights a pejorative aspect of sympathy mixed with feelings of superiority (if not contempt). Yet again, the TT is adding to the cumulative misrepresentation of Saint Teresa's father. A less pejorative, and contextually more justified, particularization of 'piadad' might be 'compassion' (that is, sympathy mixed with empathy).
4. 'a slave-girl of his brother's' contains a not wholly successful particularization of 'una' as 'a slave-girl' (gratuitously implying that the female slave in question was young).
5. 'treated her' is an unduly weak generalization of 'regalaba'. A rendering such as 'made a fuss of her', or 'pampered her' is more literally exact without any loss of idiomaticity or contextual plausibility.
6. 'his own children' is a particularizing translation; the more literally exact 'his children' would, without the emphasizing function of the added 'own', fail to bring out the point of the ST with sufficient clarity.
7. 'bear the pain of' is an unnecessarily elaborate circumlocutory particularization of 'sufrir'; 'the pain of' seems both redundant and overstated.
8. The TT has omitted a rendering of 'de piadad'; it might be advisable to avoid this generalization by adding 'out of compassion'.

Ed. TT: My father was a man of devoutest charity towards the poor, and of great compassion towards the sick, and even towards slaves; so much so that he could never bring himself to own any, because he felt such compassion for them. Once, when a female slave belonging to one of his brothers was staying in the house, he pampered her like one of his own children. He used to say that, out of compassion, he could not bear seeing her deprived of her freedom.

ST 15–16 Era de gran... gran manera.

1. 'was never heard' is a successful generalization, and grammatical transposition, of 'jamás nadie le oyó'; for reasons of TL idiomaticity, this option is clearly preferable to 'no one ever heard him'.
2. 'jurar' is a problematic word to translate: although in modern contexts it tends to be used as a literal equivalent of 'to swear (an oath)', in this text the more

Practical 7

biblical sense of 'to bear false witness' (as in the Mosaic commandment) is likely to have been intended.
3 'murmurar' presents a translation problem: there is no English word with an equally wide literal sense (which covers 'grumble, gossip, speak evil/ill of, criticize'), which makes particularization inevitable in the TT. The difficulty for the translator is to decide which of the particular senses is most likely to be contextually appropriate. In our view, 'speak slander' may be unduly particularizing, since it refers exclusively to spreading malicious untruths; our interpretation assumes that 'ni murmurar' includes not speaking ill of people even when it is true.
4 'most rigid' is a gratuitous particularization that further adds to the cumulative distortion of the description of Saint Teresa's father in the TT. The ST does not justify the impression of narrow-minded prudery ascribed to him in the TT.
5 'chastity' is at best a gross particularization, but contextually more like a mistranslation, of 'honesto'. Especially in context with 'en gran manera', 'honesto' covers a whole host of fine and upstanding qualities, of which chastity is only one.

Ed. TT: He was a very truthful man, never given to false witness or malicious gossip. He had the very highest moral standards.

NB For this exercise, you were asked to concentrate exclusively on how closely the TT has rendered the literal meaning of the ST. This is why we have gone into such detail in our commentary. Normally, when you are asked to evaluate a TT, literal meaning will be only one of many considerations to take into account, and you will only need to discuss these issues at points where literal meaning poses significant translation problems.

PRACTICAL 7

7.2 Speed translation

Assignment

In a time limit set by your tutor, produce an accurate and stylistically appropriate translation of all or part of the following ST.

Contextual information

The text is from the 1991–1992 annual supplement to the *Enciclopedia universal ilustrada Europeo-Americana* published by Espasa Calpe. It is the first section of a longer entry under the heading 'Antártida: el séptimo continente'.

Text

ANTÁRTIDA:
EL SÉPTIMO CONTINENTE

SUMARIO: *Unos datos necesarios. – La cumbre antártica de Madrid. – Las aguas de la Antártida. – El retroceso de los glaciares. – La vida del Universo a través de la Antártida. – La presencia científica española: 'Hespérides'. – Los peligros latentes. – Bibliografía.*

Fue el científico francés Jacques-Yves Cousteau quien definió la Antártida como el Séptimo Continente (el sexto sería el mar). La Antártida ha sido también definida como el Continente Helado, el Continente Deshabitado y el Continente sin Tiempo, siendo esta última versión poetizada por el escritor chileno Pablo Neruda: él le llamó también la 'catedral del hielo'. Lugar mítico, esa inmensa región despoblada se ha convertido en los últimos años en el símbolo del porvenir del planeta y es, al mismo tiempo, el celoso guardián de secretos: bajo sus enormes e impresionantes capas de hielo se encuentra la historia del clima del planeta Tierra, que es lo mismo que afirmar que retiene, y un día explicará, los secretos del origen y la evolución de la vida.

El descubrimiento del valor científico de la Antártida como testimonio de la historia de la Tierra es uno de los motivos de la reactualización de su existencia, aunque no el único. Otro motivo, de naturaleza inquietante, ha resituado también la actualidad de la Antártida entre los temas de preocupación mundial: la presencia, desde hace unos años, de un 'agujero' en el ozono que en los cielos antárticos protege la vida de las letales radiaciones ultravioleta que alcanzan nuestro planeta con la llegada de la luz y la energía solares, radiaciones que la capa de ozono, hoy dañada, retiene como función protectora.

El 1 de diciembre de 1959 fue firmado en Washington, la capital de Estados Unidos, el llamado Tratado de la Antártida, según el cual se otorgaba a este continente el estatuto de 'internacional', es decir, una tierra (helada, por supuesto) abierta a la colonización. Las naciones signatarias fueron: Argentina, Australia, Bélgica, Chile, Francia, Japón, Nueva Zelanda, Noruega, República de Sudáfrica, Gran Bretaña, Estados Unidos y la Unión Soviética. Acordaron también que esa 'colonización' debería tener unas características especiales: el uso pacífico de sus espacios, prohibición de efectuar pruebas atómicas y de enterrar residuos industriales, químicos o de cualquier tipo, y libertad de acción para la actividad científica. El tratado indicaba, asimismo, que cualquier nación interesada, al margen de las firmantes, en esa labor científica, podría tener acceso a la región, de la que, sin embargo, quedaban excluidas todas apetencias o reivindicaciones territoriales.

Reprinted by kind permission from *Enciclopedia Universal Ilustrada Europeo-Americana, Suplemento Anual, 1991–1992* (Madrid: Espasa-Calpe, 1993, p. 45), copyright © Editorial Espasa-Calpe.

Practical 8

NOTES FOR TUTORS

8.1 Connotative meaning

This assignment is best done at home, by students working individually. The commentary on pp. 60–63 may be reproduced for distribution to students at a suitable point in the discussion in Practical 8.

8.2 Connotative meaning

This assignment works well in class. Occasionally students need to be reminded of the importance of phonic/graphic and metric features whose function is to reinforce the mood created in the text by connotative means. These reinforcing features pose an obvious challenge for translators: for instance, in line 3, the marked recurrence of the vowel 'a' produces a special effect whereby the existing visual impression of a seascape blurred by a heavy heat-haze is heightened.

When setting the assignment it is essential to remind students that many expressions in a given text arguably fall into two or more categories of connotative meaning. The suggestions in our commentary on pp. 64–68 which may be reproduced for distribution to students, are certainly open to discussion. Just as the assignment on the Teresa de Jesús passage in Practical 7 was intended to make students sensitive to degrees of correspondence in literal meaning, this assignment is intended to sensitize them to the variety of types and effects of connotative meaning. In that sense, this assignment, too, is an artificial exercise: in a more global assessment of texts, neither this amount of detail nor this degree of precision in labelling categories of connotation would be expected. In short, it is important not to let students become discouraged by the complexity of the analysis of connotative meaning: the assignment is not intended as a training in taxonomy, but as a consciousness-raising exercise designed to improve sensitivity and accuracy in translation.

PRACTICAL 8

8.1 Connotative meaning

COMMENTARY ON CONNOTATIVE MEANINGS IN THE EXTRACT FROM *YERMA*

lines 3–4   The image evoked by the ST relies heavily on the *associative meaning* of 'caracoles'. The word literally refers to a snail or shell, but, by association, it is also used to refer to the shape of a spiral. The ST's connotative effects also derive partly from a textual echo of the collocation 'subir en caracol' which describes an upward spiralling movement. Thus *collocative meaning*, in the form of the subversion and distortion of a set phrase, plays a connotative role in 'le subían los caracoles'. The TT's use of the simile 'like a snail' introduces an inappropriate *associative meaning*: it evokes, instead of the spiral shape of the shell, the slimy, sluglike body of a snail. This connotation is further reinforced by the *collocative meaning* of 'curled', with the effect that, rather than suggesting an idea of water welling upwards in spirals, the TT invites the reader to imagine the movement of the water by analogy with the sluggish crawling of snail.

line 7–8   The connotative effects of this line are compounded of *reflected*, *associative* and *collocative meaning*. The literal meaning of 'fire' coexists in the ST with a figurative *reflected meaning* ('ardour'), which, by stereotypical association, connotes a manner indicative of passion or sexual arousal. Both the literal and the figurative meanings are reinforced by the collocative echoes of the set phrase 'dar fuego' ('to set on fire') which has been subverted and distorted into 'le daban fuego a'. Line 8 provides a contrast to 'fuego' in 'temblor', the latter conveying by *associative meaning* the notion of excited shivering; the alternation between 'hot' and 'cold' suggests a further *associative meaning* of feverish arousal. The TT inverts the ST order and loses

Practical 8

line 9
the contrast suggesting fever and arousal; to British readers at least it merely suggests that the woman is shivering because the air is chilly. The *associative meaning* of 'desnuda' hints at vulnerability, lack and passivity. This is reinforced by the *collocative* tendency of 'desnudo' to appear in phrases denoting a notion of 'being bereft of something' (as in 'estar desnudo de...'), and by the *reflected meaning* of 'desnudar' in the sense of 'to denude' or its figurative sense 'to ruin/break'. While, by association, 'naked' does convey something of the ST's connotation of vulnerability, this connotation is not sufficiently reinforced in the TT and is practically lost as a result.

line 10
The choice of 'doncella' from among a whole list of alternatives that could have been used here is textually significant. By stereotypical *association* this word connotes virginity. Equally stereotypical is the positive valuation that is attached to it in terms of *attitudinal meaning*. On a connotative level, the literal rendering of 'doncella' as 'maiden' constitutes a translation loss. Although the *associative meaning* of virginity is retained in the TT, the archaic and pseudo-poetic register to which the word 'maiden' belongs interferes with the conveying of a favourable *attitudinal meaning*. In any case, 'maiden' does not, in English, carry an unambiguously positive *attitudinal meaning*.

line 11
The *associative meaning* of 'se quejaba' consists in a notion of bemoaning one's fate. Apart from questions of literal inexactitude ('quejarse' normally denotes a continuous groaning, moaning or whimpering sound), the TT's choice of 'wept' is also connotatively deficient: at best it suggests the shedding of silent tears.

line 12
Reflected meaning operates through the interplay between literal (physical) and figurative (psychological) senses of 'marchita'; the ST also creates a connotative effect by the *collocative* strangeness and ambiguity of the phrase 'marchita de amores'. These connotative effects are lost from the TT.

line 16
The ST contains a play on the literal and figurative senses of 'seco', combining through *reflected meaning* the senses of both 'dried up/shrivelled' and 'barren'. In terms of both *attitudinal* and *affective meaning* 'vientre seco' carries pejorative overtones: that is, it conveys a sense of censure and disfavour both with regard to the referent (the woman's womb) and the person addressed (the woman). None of these connotative overtones are conveyed in the TT.

line 17
The ST's choice of 'quebrada' carries an *associative meaning* of unhealthiness, and possibly also a pejorative *attitudinal meaning*. These connotations are absent in the TT, which at best carries a suggestion of ageing or sudden illness as its *associative meaning*, with perhaps a hint of sympathy as its *attitudinal meaning*.

line 20
For culture-specific reasons, the *associative meaning* of 'romería' is extremely hard to convey in an English TT: the term has the religious

Thinking Spanish Translation Teachers' Handbook

associations of a pilgrimage, with the secular associations of a country fair or 'fiesta' and the sexual associations of a carnival. In context, both the devotional and the sexual connotations are clearly salient in the ST. The TT only conveys the religious associations. In addition to this, the use of the term 'romería' in a context evoking the traditional sexual love lyric in Spanish carries with it allusive connotations. This *allusive meaning* further reinforces the association of lovers' rendezvous.

line 25 The word 'chorro' carries an *associative meaning* suggestive of a narrow stream of water issuing from a constricted source and therefore flowing with some force, a connotation which is reinforced by an onomatopoeic phonic form. The TT's 'waterfall' is defective both in its *associative meaning* and in phonic reinforcement.

line 31 The *associative meanings* of 'amapola' and 'clavel' are evocative of the colour of the flowers in bloom (red), and, indirectly, of blood. They bear symbolic meanings of passionate love and carry a strong association of sexual flowering and receptiveness, which are particularly relevant in context (see the link with 'tu vientre se abra' in line 34). While less strikingly effective, the literal renderings 'carnation' and 'poppy' convey connotations of sexual flowering; however, associations of passionate love are lacking from the TT.

line 32 The connotations of 'macho', as opposed to 'hombre', create particular difficulties in an English translation: there is probably no English word with the appropriate *associative meanings* of male animality. The fact that, in this case, the speaking character is using 'el macho' to refer to himself has given the translator a way of sidestepping the connotative issue. For the audience of the play, however, the personal pronoun 'I' carries none of the stereotypical connotations evoked by 'macho' in the ST. In the ST, 'capa' has its literal meaning of 'cloak', but the use of the verb 'desplegar' gives it an *associative meaning* of 'bullfighter's cape' (cf. the bullfighting associations of carnations [line 31]).

line 34 The *associative meaning* of 'tu vientre se abra' links back to the connotations of sexual flowering and receptiveness noted in line 31. In this case the translator has made these connections more openly explicit (and therefore less subtle) than they are in the ST.

lines 35–36 By culturally stereotypical *association* 'un velo de luto' connotes widowhood, mourning and, indirectly, the negation of sexual flowering and receptiveness. The TT has made some of these tacit hints plainly explicit by its reference to 'widow's veil'. The connotations of 'dulce camisa de holanda' are placed in opposition with those of 'un velo de luto': these are *associations* of soft and pliant femininity, the sexual receptiveness of a bride on the night of her honeymoon. The choice of 'linen' detracts from the connotations of softness in the

Practical 8

TT, though the *associations* of pliant bridal femininity are not altogether lost.

Suggested TTs of the highlighted sections:

lines 3–4	Welling up around her body Spirals of water swirled.
lines 7–8	set her laughter on fire and sent a shiver down her spine
lines 9–10	Oh how bereft and naked that maid bathed in the stream!
line 11	Oh, how she moaned!
line 12	Alas, withered of loves!
lines 16–17	Alas, for her barren womb and her colour fading and wan!
line 20	When the night of the pilgrimage comes...
lines 24–25	See how dark are the waters of the mountain cascade.
lines 31–32	Carnation and red rose you'll be when the male unfurls his cloak.
lines 34–37	If you come as a pilgrim to pray for your womb to open, don't you put on your widow's weeds, but wear a soft bridal chemise.

PRACTICAL 8

8.2 Connotative meaning

COMMENTARY ON CONNOTATIVE MEANINGS IN 'SINFONÍA EN GRIS MAYOR'

title   The *associative* meaning of 'sinfonía' suggests an analogic link between sound and visual image which is crucial to the text as a whole; this link between sound and vision is further reinforced by subverting the clichéd musical collocation 'en G mayor' to create 'en gris mayor' (whose *collocative* meaning continues to echo the meaning of the musical term). The title establishes the importance of colours, particularly of various shades of grey, in the ST. It is also linked, by *allusive* meaning, to the nineteenth-century French poem 'Symphonie en blanc majeur' by Théophile Gautier, which is similarly based on an analogy between sound and colour.

line 1   'cristal azogado'
'Cristal' carries *associative* connotations (of translucence; of something bright and shimmering) and, alongside its primary meaning of 'crystal', a secondary *reflected* meaning of 'glass/mirror'; it is the combination with 'azogado' that makes 'mirror' the preferred interpretation of 'cristal' in the ST context.

Suggested TT: 'mirror backed with quicksilver'.

line 2   'la lámina... de zinc'
Particularly in context with one another, 'lámina' and 'zinc' (drawn from a technical register), are suggestive of the viewpoint of a scientifically objective observer; this *attitudinal* meaning contrasts with the impressionistic and neo-romantic features of the poem, and has a 'de-romanticising' effect in the ST.

Suggested TT: 'the zinc-plated sheet'.

Practical 8

line 3   'manchan'
By virtue of *associative* meaning this word is suggestive of flecks of dirt; there is also a hint, through a combination of *reflected* meaning ('to soil/stain') and *collocative* meaning ('to smudge'), of a pejorative *attitudinal* meaning which contrasts with the clichéd 'romantic' attitude to birds.

Suggested TT: 'make a smudge'.

line 4   'el fondo bruñido de pálido gris'
There is a connotative clash of practically oxymoronic proportions between the *associative* meaning of 'bruñido' (connoting shiny brightness) and the *associative* meaning of 'pálido' (connoting colourlessness); 'el fondo' must not be taken here as elliptical of the collocation 'el fondo del mar' ('the bottom of the sea'): its appropriate literal meaning in context with describing the sky is 'background', with *associative* meanings linked to notions of the background of a painting, or of a stage-set.

Suggested TT: 'the burnished backdrop with its pale shade of grey'.

line 6   'con paso de enfermo'
There is a collocative clash between this phrase, connoting by *associative* meaning a personification of the sun as a sick old man, and 'como un vidrio' whose *associative* meaning presents the sun as an inanimate object: the overall effect is oxymoronic.

Suggested TT: 'shuffles with infirm steps'.

line 8   'su negro clarín'
This is an unexpected and somewhat opaque collocation, carrying a number of connotations: by virtue of *collocative* meaning it suggests a personification of 'el viento', by *associative* meaning it recalls the cherubic representation of the wind seen on old maps; 'negro', with its evident colour connotations, forms a notably unexpected collocation with 'clarín' whose normal *associative* meaning is the colour of brass.

Suggested TT: 'its black clarion'

line 9   'su vientre de plomo'
While this phrase will probably cause no significant problems of translation, it is worth noting that here again the ST manifests a collocative clash (in the form of oxymoronic connotations): 'vientre', by virtue of *associative* meaning, presents 'las ondas' as an animate being; 'plomo', by virtue of its *associative* meaning, presents them as inanimate. (In terms of the overall 'colour-scheme' of the poem, 'plomo' is also connotatively significant.)

Thinking Spanish Translation Teachers' Handbook

Suggested TT: 'their bellies of lead'

line 13 'vago, lejano, brumoso país'
The combined *associative* meanings of the adjectives qualifying 'país' hint at the notion of an indistinctly seen (or remembered) landscape: a suggestion of mystery, as well as an image of a misty scene whose greyness contrasts with the heat-haze of the tropics, form part of this complex of connotations.

Suggested TT: 'faraway, misty, mysterious land'.

line 14 'lobo'
This is a truncated version of the cliché 'lobo de mar' and should be understood in terms of this *allusive* meaning ('sea dog/old salt').

Suggested TT: 'old salt'.

'tostaron'
Its obvious colour associations apart, the term has evident culinary connotations, the most contextually relevant of these being the *collocative* echo of 'to roast coffee' (note the stereotypical association between coffee and the 'Brasil' of line 15).

Suggested TT: 'roasted'.

line 15 'fuego'
The *associative* meaning of flames adds yet another touch of colour to the ST, and links at the same time with the culinary associations of 'tostaron'; it may not be too far fetched to suggest that, by a combination of *reflected* and *allusive* meaning, the text indirectly evokes 'Tierra del Fuego' (a connotation that is almost inevitably bound to be lost in an English TT).

Suggested TT: 'burning, fiery'

line 17 'frasco de gin'
As a loan word from English, 'gin' connotes, by *associative* meaning, a notion of foreignness that reinforces the globe-trotting experiences of the old seaman; in an English TT, 'gin' might convey inappropriate cultural associations ('mother's ruin', 'gin and tonic'): it might usefully be replaced by the name of a drink with more exotic, seafaring and tropical connotations.

Suggested TT: 'bottle of rum'.

line 18 'impregnada de yodo y salitre'
In a manner similar to 'la lámina... de zinc' (line 2), this phrase (with its vocabulary drawn from a technical register) is suggestive of an

Practical 8

attitude of objective observation: an *attitudinal* meaning that clashes incongruously with 'roja nariz', creating an effect of bathos and irony.

Suggested TT: 'saturated with brine and iodine'

line 22   'humo que forma el tabaco'
By means of the visual aspect of the *associative* meaning of this phrase yet another shade of grey (contrasting with the tropical haze and with the grey of the 'brumoso país') is connotatively introduced into the text.

Suggested TT: 'curling smoke from his pipe'.

line 24   'dorada'
Once again, *associative* meaning, in the form of colour connotations, is used to inject yet another contrasting colour into the visual mix created in the ST; 'dorada' also conveys a positive *attitudinal* meaning, enhancing in this instance, a mood of dreamy nostalgia.

Suggested TT: 'golden'.

line 25   'bergantín'
By *associative* meaning this word conjures up something of the romantic image of a sailing-ship with white sails (this romantic feature stands in significant contrast with items of down-to-earth and 'de-romanticised' description elsewhere in the text, for instance 'su blusa de dril' in line 21).

Suggested TT: 'brig'.

line 27   'gama'
Conveys a complex of *associative* and *reflected* meanings in which the elements of music (scale) and colour (spectrum) are combined.

Suggested TT: 'scale'.

line 28   'esfumino'
Literally, this refers to a brush, eraser or rag used in painting for rubbing down hard lines or blending the lines of shading (used here to create a simile referring to the blurring of the line of the horizon); by virtue of its *associative* meaning 'esfumino' reiterates the motif of painting in the ST (see 'el fondo' in line 4; note also that Darío's own conception of the poem was that of 'painting with words'). The main translation problem is that the English technical term for 'esfumino' is 'stump': a word which will almost certainly be misunderstood by most English readers, and which also carries altogether the wrong set of connotations (stunted growth, severed limbs, broken tree-trunk/mast, and so on).

Thinking Spanish Translation Teachers' Handbook

Suggested TT: 'brushstroke'.

line 29   'borrara'
In *associative* meaning this word reiterates a connotative motif found in the 'manchan' of line 3 (the notion of a smudge or smear); by implication there is a hint of a pejorative *attitudinal* meaning here which may be said to have a 'de-romanticising' effect (also noted elsewhere in the text).

Suggested TT: 'blotted out'.

line 30   'cigarra'
In terms of *associative* meaning, 'cigarra' is practically a cliché of tropical local colour; this, however, is equally true of English 'cicada'.

line 31   'senil'
By *associative* meaning this reiterates the motif of age and infirmity found in line 6.

Suggested TT: 'doddering'.

lines 32–33   'solo monótono... su violín'
May be said to constitute an echo, by *allusive* meaning, of Paul Verlaine's lines: 'Les sanglots longs / Des violons / De l'automne / Blessent mon cœur / D'une langueur / Monotone.' Unless the English reader is familiar with French poetry, this allusion is likely to be lost in the TT; however, the same consideration holds for Spanish readers of the ST.

Practical 9

NOTES FOR TUTORS

9.1 Language variety: dialect and sociolect

This assignment is best done in class. Ideally, students should listen to the recording (probably twice) before following it on the printed transcript which is given on p. 72 and may be reproduced for distribution in class. Listening to the recording without the aid of the printed text allows students to concentrate on the prominent dialectal and sociolectal features of the oral text without being distracted by the vagaries of the spelling in the transcript. The idea is not to score points by guessing the speaker's provenance, but to assess how far and in what ways his speech diverges from standard Spanish, and to try to make sense of what he is saying. Of course, students are not expected to be experts on Spanish dialects, and should not be made to feel inadequate if they experience difficulties with understanding the dialect speaker on tape. (Working together in groups helps to alleviate this problem.) The interviewee in this recording is a fisherman from the Andalusian dialect area.

After briefly discussing the dialectal and sociolectal features that can be discerned from listening to the text, students can be handed the transcript and given the opportunity to listen to the recording again, following it on the transcript. They can then move on to attempting what actually amounts to an intralingual translation into standard Spanish. (A more standard Spanish rendering of the text is given on p. 73 and can be reproduced for distribution to students after their own versions have been discussed.) By this stage of the assignment both a full comprehension of the text and a full appreciation of its dialectal and sociolectal features should be assured and students should be ready to move on to the final stage of producing an English TT suitable for voice-over purposes.

The entire assignment can be completed in about an hour.

Practical 9

9.2 Language variety: code-switching

This is another assignment that works well in class and it can be completed in about 45 minutes. The only point on which students may need reassurance is the actual code-switching, which in this text is that of the novelist, not of the individual characters. This is an important distinction to make, since in other cases code-switching may occur in the speech of one and the same speaker.

PRACTICAL 9

9.1 Language variety: dialect and sociolect

TRANSCRIPT OF TAPED EXTRACT 'EL SUSTO MÁS GRANDE...'

Text

El zuhto má' grande, pue' le voy a decir una coza: el zuhto má' grande hace cuestión de treinta y do' ó treinta y tre' año'. Veniámo' de Málaga, qu' estábamo' pe'cando en Málaga. Y yo llevo ya en un bode luh má' de... má' de cuarenta año', en un bode luh, e' el que trae el pezcao, en un bode luh. Ya llegando a mi caza, viendo yo mi caza ya, allí en Almuñécar, donde tú me ha' dicho hoy que... 'de está,...'de está 'El Moro', allí enfrente...
   – ¿El Criztóba'?
   – El Criztóba'. Vino un golpe de mar, puzo el bode boca abao y me pilló debao. Y a la de tre' o cuatro vez – claro, yo tenía veinte ciete año' cuando ezo. Si fuera sido hoy, pue' me fuera ahogao. Lo que paza, que yo todavía pueh, no, no e' lo mi'mo. Y yo decía pa' mí, y digo: '¡Digo! ¡Y que yo...! ¡Que viendo yo mi caza, qu' me... que me tenga yo que ahogar aquí!' Y a la de tre' vecez de campuzá, ¿zabez tú? Me quité la ropa tó. Me lo arranqué tó. Y tiré a la mar toíca la ropa de arriba. Tó lo que llevaba – y fue en el mez, en el mez prócimo a la Pazcua, y tó me lo quité, y... y lo tiré tó. Tó me lo arranqué.

Llegué a mi caza, y mi mujer no había enterao. Dice mi mujer: '¿Pero qué e' lo que ha' hecho con la ropa? ¡Viene'... viene' goteando!'. Digo: '¿Que qué?' 'Pue' miralo, 'papao.' 'Ha venido un golpe de mar y ha puezto el bode boga abao.'

        (Transcription by Maggie Bolton)

Practical 9

STANDARD VERSION OF
TAPED EXTRACT 'EL SUSTO MÁS GRANDE...'

Text

El susto más grande, pues le voy a decir una cosa: el susto más grande hace cuestión de 32 o 33 años, veníamos de Málaga, que estábamos pescando en Málaga. Y yo llevo ya en un bote luz más de, más de 40 años (en un bote luz, el que trae el pescado), en un bote luz. Y ya llegando a mi casa, viendo yo mi casa ya, allí en Almuñécar, donde tú me has dicho hoy que... donde está, donde está 'El Moro', allí enfrente....
 – ¿El Cristóbal?
 – El Cristóbal. Vino un golpe de mar, puso el bote boca abajo y me pilló debajo. Y a la de tres o cuatro veces. Claro, yo tenía 27 años cuando eso. Si hubiera sido hoy, pues me habría ahogado. Lo que pasa, que yo todavía pues, no, no es lo mismo. Y yo decía para mí, y digo: '¡Digo! ¡Y que yo...!, ¡y que viendo yo mi casa, que me tenga yo que ahogar aquí!' Y a la de tres veces de campuzada, ¿sabes tú? Me quité la ropa, todo. Me lo arranqué todo. Y tiré a la mar todita la ropa de arriba. Todo lo que llevaba – y fue en el mes, en el mes próximo a la Pascua – y todo me lo quité. Y lo... y lo tiré todo. Todo me lo arranqué.
 Llegué a mi casa, y mi mujer no se había enterado. Dice mi mujer: '¿Pero qué es lo que has hecho con la ropa? ¡Vienes... vienes goteando!' Digo: '¿Que qué?' 'Pues míralo, empapado.' 'Ha venido un golpe de mar y ha puesto el bote boca abajo.'

Adapted from *Voces Hispánicas; Spoken Documents for Advanced Learners of Spanish*, compiled by María Fernández Toro (London: Birkbeck College, p. 43), copyright © Birkbeck College.

Practical 10

NOTES FOR TUTORS

10.1 Language variety: social register and tonal register

This assignment is best done at home. Students should be reminded that their prime focus should be on features of social and tonal register, just as ours is in the commentary on pp. 76–80. (This commentary may be reproduced for distribution to students at a suitable point in the Practical.)

The very fact that social register and tonal register are intermingled ingredients in the style of a text makes it important to try to distinguish them from one another. The more accurately translators see which of these features is operative, in what proportions, and to what effect, the more informed their decisions of detail will be in formulating a TT. As at several other junctures in the course, students should be reassured here that they are being initiated into an operation which may at first seem excessively laborious, but which, with practice, can become as much a matter of reflex as driving a car.

10.2 Language variety: dialect, social register and tonal register

Before going on to the actual assignment, students might be given an opportunity to listen to and discuss briefly the two recordings transcribed on p. 121 of the coursebook. The speaker of *Text 1* is from Spain and is designated as 'la responsable del departmento de la mujer del sindicato Unión General de Trabajadores'; *Text 2* is spoken by a well-travelled and educated woman from Venezuela.

The actual assignment, which is particularly designed for group work in class, is similar to the assignment in the first part of Practical 9 – with the major difference that, in formulating a TT, students are expected to place greater emphasis on conveying the speaker's social and tonal register. There are elements of humour in the ST which should, ideally, not be lost in an effective TT.

After listening to the recording (perhaps twice) and holding a short discussion on the salient features of language variety, social register, and tonal register that

Practical 10

can be discerned, students should be handed copies of the transcript (the text on p. 82) and given the opportunity to listen to the recording again, following the spoken text in the transcript. At this stage, students should be asked to pick out the non-standard features of the oral text on tape: a good way of doing this is by (a) highlighting discrepancies between the transcript and what the speaker actually says, and (b) noting discrepancies between what the speaker says, and what a standard Spanish rendering might be. (The speaker in this extract, identified as 'Elizabeth', comes from Chile.) Before going on to the final part of the assignment, students should be asked to comment on the degree to which they perceive the spoken ST to differ from European Spanish. In subsequent discussion of their voice-over TTs, it is important to consider the issue of the use of non-standard features of English, the question of what variety of English (if any) was used, and the proportion of markedly non-standard features in the TT. This aspect of the assignment can be linked to the issue of textual genre (in particular, oral versus written genres) discussed in Chapters 11 and 12.

PRACTICAL 10

10.1 Language variety: social register and tonal register

**COMMENTARY ON LANGUAGE VARIETY IN THE
EXTRACT FROM *LA VIDA ES SUEÑO***

(i) Salient features

The most salient features of this text can be divided into three categories: first, the manipulation of verse form; second, the choice of lexis; and finally, the alternation of mode of address between 'vos' (an honorific form equivalent to modern 'usted') and 'tú'. All three of these techniques convey information about the social and tonal registers of the characters who utter them: in fact, the ST contains a number of the features described in Chapter 9 of the course-book, among them code-switching.

The verse form which Calderón employs in *La vida es sueño* is *redondillas* (a stanza comprising four octosyllabic lines), the unity of which is reinforced through the use of *rima abrazada* (abba). A cursory glance at the ST extract will be enough to draw the student's attention to the distribution of lines and stanzas amongst the characters. Estrella speaks whole lines, and Astolfo – apart from the aside in line 2 – also speaks in whole lines. In contrast to this, the Second Manservant and Segismundo are assigned parts of lines and the flow of stanzas is broken up in their speeches, particularly during their altercation. This can be seen readily in the following lines, in which the rhyme words are 'así', 'digo', 'conmigo' and 'mí':

> CRIADO 2º   [...] que no
>   es justo atreverse así,
>   y estando Astolfo...
> SEGISMUNDO   ¿No digo
>   que vos no os metáis conmigo?
> CRIADO 2º   Digo lo que es justo.
> SEGISMUNDO   A mí [...]

The textual characteristic of varying the extent to which whole lines and stanzas

Practical 10

are attributed to individual characters is employed to suggest the social affiliations of the characters, and more particularly to convey the fact that Segismundo is associated with the rustic and uncouth. Furthermore, Segismundo's sarcastic use of a whole stanza (discussed below) at lines 29–32 illustrates that he is capable of affecting a higher social register, if only in order to mimic one of the other characters. In the light of this, Calderón's manipulation of verse form can be seen to contribute to the social registers employed by the characters who appear in the extract.

Just as Calderón uses verse form as a feature of social register, he uses lexis to suggest the tonal register employed. A particularly apposite example of both of these features may be found in the final stanza of the extract, in which Segismundo uses an entire stanza of end-stopped lines in mimicry of the affected courtly tone used by Astolfo. He contrasts this with lexical content which begins in a high register ('tan severo', 'hablar con entereza') but which then shifts to a somewhat circumlocutory but yet crude threat, 'quizá no hallaréis cabeza/en que se os tenga el sombrero' which is nonetheless couched, also sarcastically, in the 'vos' form of address. Further examples of the use of 'vos' versus 'tú' will be discussed as they occur.

(ii) Specific details

We give here a list of particular ST expressions that are marked as features of social register and/or tonal register and would require attention in translating. (Our suggested TTs are accompanied by two important provisos. First, these TTs are not intended to read as verse: the constraints of translation into verse often entail widespread compensation in place, and the whole text would need to be translated for the rendering of any given line to be convincing. Second, in our TTs we have not taken up the very real option of compensation by adding stage directions as a means of making sure the actors speak their lines in the right tone.)

line 1   'Séd más galán cortesano'
Indicative of the sociolect of the courtier, Estrella addresses Segismundo as 'vos' thereby suggesting his superiority as her prince. Her choice of vocabulary indicates a courtly social register; however, her appeal for Segismundo to improve his behaviour suggests a slighty chastising tonal register, modified by the extent to which she presents herself as aware of his social superiority. The tone of respect is perhaps best conveyed through the use of a term such as 'sir' or 'lord'.

Suggested TT: I pray you, my lord, be more courteous.

line 5   'Advierte, señor'
The Second Manservant uses the term 'señor' to reinforce Segismundo's social superiority. The usual semantic field of 'to warn' is too strong for rendering 'advertir' here, given the position of respect

Thinking Spanish Translation Teachers' Handbook

which the speaker takes up when addressing Segismundo, and therefore 'advise' or 'suggest' might be tonally more appropriate.

Suggested TT: If I may advise you, my lord

lines 10, 13 'justo'
& 16 This term forms part of a word system evident in this extract which is associated with correct courtly behaviour, and which is thematically related to Segismundo's treatment and condition as a nobleman who has been isolated from courtly practices. Calderón manipulates the noun by emphasizing different aspects of its semantic field (its cultural aspect when used by the Manservant, its aspect based in human nature when taken up by Segismundo), finally bringing it to rhyme position in line 10 where it forms the central couplet of a *redondilla*, and the semantic shift is reinforced by the rhyme 'justo/gusto'. Although 'just' offers an appealing translation, 'right' may in fact underscore the thematic link of nature versus culture more readily and more idiomatically.

Suggested TTs: It is not right to carry on in that way.
I am only telling you what is right.
If it's not to *my* taste, it can't be right.

lines 8–9 ¿No digo / que vos no os metáis conmigo?
In semantic content these lines convey an unveiled threat: this clashes in tone with Segismundo's use of the honorific 'vos'. The clash suggests the social stereotyping of Segismundo as caustic. In addition to this he is adopting a sarcastic tonal register.

Suggested TT: And *I*, my good sir, am only telling *you* to mind your own business.

lines 15–16 Pues yo, señor, he escuchado / de ti
The servant responds to Segismundo's sarcastic rejoinder by employing a similar clash of lexis and tonal register. He picks up on Segismundo's code-switching and replicates it by dropping the courtly 'vos' formula, used by other speakers to address Segismundo, in favour of 'tú'. However, he maintains a semblance of respect in his use of the deferential term 'señor'.

Suggested TT: Well, *sir*, I have heard you say

lines 21–22 'Con los hombres como yo / no puede hacerse eso'
The servant is claiming a degree of social status which – considering he is addressing a prince – he may well not enjoy. He therefore is presented as being presumptuous and somewhat self-regarding.

Suggested TT: You cannot do that to a man like me.

Practical 10

**lines 24
& 29**   '¡Por Dios que lo he de probar!' and '¡vive Dios que pudo ser!'
The comic effect of Segismundo throwing an uppity servant over the balcony is underscored by the parallel references to God in each of these lines, both of which refer to the possibility of Segismundo being able to carry out the threat. They serve, of course, to continue the social stereotyping of Segismundo as aggressive and unaware of the boundaries of behaviour becoming to a prince. They should be rendered in a way which manifests the fact they are parallel. (Note that the play on 'poder', consisting of a shift from its cultural to its natural, physical aspect, parallels the shift between two aspects of 'justo', as discussed above.)

Suggested TTs: Let's damn' well see, by God!
You see, it could be done, by God!

lines 30–33   A whole quatrain is spoken by Astolfo who uses formal end-stopped lines. In his speech the formal tone is re-established through use of the 'vos' form.

line 30   'Pues medid con más espacio'
Astolfo's warning to Segismundo may in fact be word-play on 'medir' (to weigh up; to scan or measure [a line of verse]). Segismundo picks up this exhortation by replying (at lines 31–33) with a similarly formal quatrain.

lines 32–33   Astolfo's reference to 'de hombres a fieras' and 'desde un monte a palacio' is a deliberate allusion to the fact that Segismundo acts in an uncouth fashion precisely because he was brought up in isolation in a tower on a mountain. In this warning, Astolfo suggests that Segismundo's innate nobility should overrule the baseness engendered by the environment in which he was brought up. In fact, immediately prior to this episode the Manservant has described Segismundo to Astolfo as 'en montes nacido'. Some form of this reference should be maintained in order to suggest Astolfo's attitude to nobility and Segismundo's inability to live up to those standards which are expected of a high-born courtier. The term 'monte' carries a significant associative meaning: it is stereotypically employed to refer to wild places, far from civilisation.

Suggested TT: Come sir, temper the brutish impulse of your actions, and know that between beast and man the distance is no less great than from mountain to palace.

line 34   'Pues en dando tan severo'
Segismundo's response begins with the same word as Astolfo's speech: he is mockingly aping Astolfo's high register and formal tone. Use of the same opening expression should therefore be maintained in an effective TT. Segismundo punningly describes Astolfo

both as being stern and as going on about the harshness of Segismundo's actions. If possible the play on words – a feature of Segismundo's social register – should be maintained or compensated for in the TT.

lines 36–37 'quizá no hallaréis cabeza / en que se os tenga el sombrero'
Segismundo's reference to Astolfo's hat is necessary to the text: it alludes to a particular hat ('el Grande') worn by Astolfo which Segismundo considers should be removed in his royal presence. This is mentioned in the scene immediately prior to the extract. The hat itself signifies Astolfo's social status. Segismundo's rather abrupt and uncouth threat conveys his anger at what he perceives to be Astolfo's presumption. The use of the deictic 'your' or 'that' may suffice to emphasize these allusions.

Suggested TT: Come sir, speak less brutally of being brutish, or you may find the gap between your neck and your hat has no head in it.

PRACTICAL 10

10.2 Language variety: dialect, social register and tonal register

TRANSCRIPT OF TAPED EXTRACT '¿CÓMO SE DISTINGUE...?'

Text

Interviewer: ¿Cómo se distingue lingüísticamente el argentino del chileno? Cuando los argentinos turistas vienen acá, ¿cómo se distinguen?
Elizabeth: Mira, en muy pocas palabras, yo te diría que el argentino habla español y el chileno canta. El argentino habla español y habla fuerte, que a mí personalmente me gusta mucho, ¿ah? El pueblo argentino 5
es un pueblo muy potente, ¿no es cierto?, y eso lo....
Interviewer: ¿Prepotente?
Elizabeth: No, ¡potente!
Interviewer: ¿Pero a veces prepotente?
Elizabeth: Yo no lo encuentro prepotente. Mira, la mayoría de los chilenos lo... 10
lo encuentra muy prepotente y aquí existe, yo percibo, un cierto complejo, ¿no es cierto? Por ejemplo, los hombres chilenos les tienen un poco como de envidia a los hombres argentinos, porque los hombres argentinos hablan más fuerte, son buenmocísimos, yo los encuentro francamente una delicia de hombres, ¿no es cierto? Son 15
mucho más altos que los chilenos, eh, es que en general el hombre chileno es... es más bajo, eh, el hombre chileno es un hombre que siente complejo frente al hombre argentino, ¿no es cierto?, porque aquí vienen mucho los argentinos a veranear, ¿no es cierto?, y las 'lolitas' chilenas se vuelven pero locas con los argentinos y con justa 20
razón, porque tienen mucha más personalidad, hablan más fuerte, son muy varoniles, ¿no es cierto?...

Adapted from *Paso Doble; a Second Stage Spanish Course on BBC Radio*, produced by Carol Stanley (London: BBC Books, 1989, p. 33). Extract reproduced from *Paso Doble* by Clare Mar Molinero with the permission of BBC Enterprises Limited.

Practical 11

NOTES FOR TUTORS

11.1 Genre

Translating song lyrics into a TT that can be sung effectively is both a challenging and an entertaining task. What is more, it is a task that forcefully illustrates the constraints genre can impose on translation strategy. Since a song, provided it is a good one, is a harmonious interweaving of text and music, a prime strategic consideration for the translator is to achieve a TT that, in its turn, successfully interweaves the verbal text with the musical score (which has to be taken as a constant). Devices that are too obviously and obtrusively contrived for making the lyrics 'fit the tune' tend to spoil this effect: they are likely to be perceived as jarring infelicities in the sung performance, or as incongruous features inviting ridicule. This may, of course, be turned to good account in the TT of a humorous song, but is bound to spoil song texts that have a serious content.

In translating 'Gracias a la vida' into a singable TT, far more attention has to be paid to the actual rhythmic patterns of the ST (especially in its sung performance) than would be the case in translating verse either for silent reading or for reading aloud. Since the TT must fit the rhythmic properties of the tune plausibly, students must familiarize themselves with the sung ST by repeated and careful listening to the recording (provided on the tape which accompanies this handbook). In doing so, they will observe that the singer takes certain liberties (mainly in the form of syllable elision and the placement of syllables sung on a long note) with the prosody that the text would have in ordinary speech. This observation justifies a degree of metrical freedom (for instance, fitting two short syllables into the space of a long musical note or stretching a single syllable over two notes) in the TT. To manipulate this degree of freedom, students need to reconstruct, if only in rudimentary form, the rhythmic patterns of the musical score. This is why we suggest doing the first part of the assignment in class, listening to the recording and performing a rhythmic analysis, before students attempt their translations at home. (On pp. 86–87 we give a singable TT of the song, for distribution to students. This version corresponds to the text as sung on tape, which differs considerably from the printed lyrics: for instance, the entire second stanza of the lyrics has been omitted. Students should be reminded that their ST is the sung performance, not the printed lyrics.)

Practical 11

No matter how good a student's TT of the song may look on paper, the ultimate test of its success must be that it can be sung to the original tune. The assignment should be rounded off by getting students to sing their TTs. If the tutor plays the guitar, so much the better, although we have found that students will enjoy using the tape as accompaniment to their TTs.

11.2 Genre

This assignment is particularly designed for group work in class, with each group reading through the entire text, but concentrating on translating one section.

In contrast to the previous assignment, this one is an exercise in constructing a TT in a specific written genre: the genre of book reviews in quality newspapers. An advantage of the choice of genre in this assignment is that students are likely to be familiar with the genre of book reviews. They should be encouraged to use their experience of this genre as guidelines for formulating a generically plausible TT. In particular, they should avail themselves of appropriate formulaic, perhaps even jargonistic, forms of expression wherever these conveniently offer themselves – for instance, 'just out', 'the recent publication of...', 'a heavy-weight volume of 780 pages'. (Of course, one must at the same time beware of turning the TT into a comic pastiche by overmarking its genre-specific features.)

Though in many respects this assignment might seem to lack the narrow constraints that specific generic needs impose on translating song lyrics, the task it sets is by no means unconstrained: in this case by plausibility in respect to register, accuracy in factual detail, and readability.

PRACTICAL 11

11.1 Genre

SONG-LYRIC ASSIGNMENT: 'GRACIAS A LA VIDA'

Sample TT

Life, I'm here to thank you for all the things you gave me.
You gave me eyes to save me from stumbling blindly.
You stop me from confusing black with white when choosing,
and help me see clearly, in starry skies reached nearly,
among all the faces the man I love so dearly.   5

Life, I'm here to thank you for all the things you gave me.
The music that you gave me, and all the words to praise you.
So in the songs I'm making I can be celebrating
brother and friend, loved dearly; mother remembered clearly,
and the bright light of the path I've climbed so sheerly.   10

Life, I'm here to thank you for all the things you gave me.
When my aching steps pained me, strength to go on came from you.
And so you've moved me onward, still striding forward,
over land, over ocean through your wild commotion:
ever nearer my lover's house drawn by your motion.   15

Life, I'm here to thank you for all the things you gave me.
The heartbeat that you gave me, that quickens when I'm near you.
And when I see creation in man's imagination,
and hear the distant singing of song-thrush homeward winging,
then when I look deep into your eyes my heart is ringing. 20

Practical 11

Life, I'm here to thank you for all the things you gave me.
I thank you for the laughter through tears and disaster.
And now I can decipher the two halves of the answer:
the song I'm singing is not just one heart ringing,
the song that sings in all of you is just the same song.　　　　25
The song I sing for all of you is just my own song.
Life, I'm here to thank you.
Life, I'm here to thank you.

Practical 12

NOTES FOR TUTORS

12.1 Subtitling

The first part of the assignment is best done by students working individually to make their own tentative cuts in the text after having listened to the recording (at least twice). Once the spottings have been discussed and agreed, the tutor can pause the recording at the end of each cut for the students to time them. Having reached a consensus on spotting and timing, students can complete the rest of the assignment by working in groups. (If time is short, the groups can be asked to complete their subtitling TTs at home and hand them in to be marked by the tutor and discussed briefly in the next Practical.)

There are two main categories of problem raised by this assignment. The first concerns a strategy for dealing with the linguistic characteristics of the ST; the second arises from the specific constraints of subtitling.

Linguistic characteristics

The first problem is that of how to handle such typically oral features of the ST as hesitations, false starts, pauses, and changes of tempo. By and large, these can be regarded as features of social register that, taken as a whole, inform the hearer of the recorded ST about the social persona projected by the speaker.

On the one hand, limitations of time (for displaying titles), of space (for showing titles on screen), and of the viewer's patience (in deciphering titles that are not easy to read) militate against reproducing these typically oral features on screen. On the other hand, a complete elimination of all features that carry information about the ST speakers' social personae would produce a colourless, uni-dimensional TT, might create a misleading impression of the speakers by failing to signal significant facts about their relative statuses, and might even clash ludicrously with the stereotyped impression of a speaker suggested to the viewer by visual clues on screen.

A compromise is probably the best solution: the text of the titles can be tidied up for the most part, but one may choose to include in it a few marks of oral styles sparingly indicative of the speakers' social registers.

Practical 12

The second strategic problem is how to handle non-standard language varieties in the ST. Probably the safest solution is not to attempt in the written titles a hint at regional accents – attempts at dialectal spellings will only make for difficulties for the viewer. On the other hand, a 'non-standard' colloquial and rural register can be suggested by a combination of contracted forms such as 'I'll', 'he'd', 'won't' (which also save space on screen) and a judicious choice of 'homely' lexical items and idioms.

Third, there is the problem of how to handle cases of textual incoherence. Particularly in a conversational setting including several interlocutors, speakers do not necessarily marshall their discourse in an ideally clear and coherent sequence. The viewer, however, does not have time to 'restructure' discourse coherence if presented with a relatively incoherent set of subtitles. It may therefore be a good idea, as suggested on p. 151 of the coursebook, to reorganize the sequence in which ideas are presented so that they form a transparently coherent set of titles.

Constraints imposed by subtitling

Many students find this assignment unexpectedly complicated. There are three especially common faults: first, a simple failure to observe the stated constraints of time and length; second, a failure to make each title comprehensible in itself; and third, a failure to make the succession of titles coherent for reading.

A good way of putting student TTs to the test is to have the students' timed subtitles typed out, laying them out as shown on p. 150 of the coursebook. Type the titles in single spacing, and leave a double space between each title. Transfer the typescript to an overhead projector transparency. Take a piece of card large enough to cover the transparency, and cut two slits in it corresponding to the two columns of typing (timings and titles). The titles slit should be exactly 36 typed spaces long and two lines deep. If the transparency is slid under the card title by title, the class can get a fair impression of how easy or difficult it is for the viewer to make sense of each title and of the whole text. Some titles simply lose their tails through amputation!

It is important to remember that moments of silence, as well as moments during which there is no title shown on screen, must be taken into account when subtitles are produced.

12.2 Speed translation

For this classroom assignment, students can be asked for either a rough draft TT or a polished one, depending on time available. The tutor may wish to specify what kind of newspaper the TT should be designed for. For the first option 15 minutes should suffice and 25 minutes for the second. In either case at least 15 minutes should be left for discussion of the TTs. The ST on pp. 90–91 may be reproduced for distribution to students. The ST is 270 words long.

PRACTICAL 12

12.2 Speed translation

Assignment

Working individually, translate the following article. Your TT should pay attention to layout as well as to accuracy. Your tutor will tell you how long you have for the exercise.

Contextual information

The article is taken from the 9 January 1993 issue of the sporting journal *AS*. The TT should be suitable for inclusion on the sports page of a newspaper.

Text

SORPRESA:
LUIS PÉREZ TITULAR

SAN SEBASTIAN
Mañu DE LA PUENTE/'Deia'

¿*VUELVE LUIS PEREZ?*

Toshack y sus futbolistas siguen preparando el encuentro dominical que les enfrenterá al Real Madrid en Atocha y en plena 'cuesta de enero'. Y lo hacen en dos frentes o de dos maneras, como se quiera. Por un lado, faenan los suplentes, y por otro, los titulares.

Aquéllos jugaron en Anglet el anunciado encuentro amistoso contra la segunda formación del Nantes. Hubo gran diferencia entre las dos formaciones y se acabó imponiendo la donostiarra por 3–0. Las dianas (dos), de Loinaz y Górriz, todas ellas de cabeza y a la salida de otros tantos córners, valieron una justa victoria. Por otro lado, el evento fue valorado como positivo por los cuatros técnicos blanquiazules, que están en disposición de repetir en cuanto se presente la ocasión.

Los titulares, por su parte, trabajaron también ayer en Atocha, y lo hicieron a puerta cerrada. De todos modos, la sesión fue observada por los periodistas desde el mercado de las Frutas. Tal observación vino a romper, de alguna manera, la casi totalidad de los planes que se han marcado los medios informativos de la capital donostiarra.

Sí, porque dio la impresión de que Toshack va a volver a contar para la titularidad con Luis Pérez, quien ayer se movió muy cerca de Kodro. Si así fuera, siempre en contra de lo pronosticado, sería Alkiza quien empezaría en el banquillo. Sería, en verdad, una gran sorpresa, pero de Toshack se puede esperar tanto lo mejor como lo peor.

Reproduced by kind permission from *AS: diario gráfico deportivo* (Madrid: Edita Semana, Sábado, 9 de enero de 1993), copyright © Edita Semana.

Practical 13

NOTES FOR TUTORS

The three technical texts used in this Practical come from three different scientific domains: archaeology, and two different branches of physics. The purpose is to introduce some breadth into our brief coverage of technical translation. Some students will be wary of these assignments, because of their ignorance of the topics covered. This is just as it should be; they should be encouraged not to guess at solutions, but to translate the texts as best they can, in consultation with specialists wherever possible. If the tutor can also consult specialists in the requisite fields, so much the better, but this is not essential – the TTs given on pp. 94–96 clear up the obscurities of construal and vocabulary. (These TTs may be reproduced for distribution to students after discussion of their own TTs.)

The assignments in this Practical work best if carried out in class, but with students having done some background preparation in advance. They should be encouraged to do some lexical research and to find their own technical consultants. The three assignments can be completed in a two-hour session, provided that the tutor keeps the pace moving along; alternatively, separate groups may be asked to work, and report back, on assignments 13.1 and 13.3.

PRACTICAL 13

13.1 Technical translation

PUBLISHED TRANSLATION OF THE ARCHAEOLOGICAL ABSTRACT

Text

The importance of preceramic remains of potatoes and sweet potatoes in the Casma valley.

This is a critical review of the existing data on potato (Solanum tuberosum) and sweet potato (Ipomoea batatas) findings in preceramic contexts of the Central Andean area. The author concludes that the only specimens having scientific validity are those found at the Huaynuma site in the Casma valley (north-central Peruvian coast), dated approximately at 2,000 years B.C.

(Bonavia, 1984, p. 20)

PRACTICAL 13

13.2   Technical translation

TRANSLATION OF THE EXTRACT FROM
THE 'CONGELACIÓN' TEXT

Text

Freezing
When salt water freezes, the fresh water forms ice crystals, while the salts remain in solution in the unfrozen water. Distillation by freezing is a two-stage process of cooling and heating. In any freezing process the temperature of salt water is lowered until ice forms. The ice is then separated from the saline solution and   5
melted to produce drinking water.

Let us now examine the general principles and operational factors on which the freezing process is based. Salt water is cooled through heat transference induced by contact with water at a lower temperature. As the water is cooled, its temperature drops until it reaches freezing point. Once freezing point is   10
reached, its temperature remains constant while cooling continues until freezing is completed. The amount of thermal energy which must be extracted from water at freezing point in order to convert it into ice is known as its latent heat of fusion, or simply latent heat. One of the principal reasons for an interest in freezing as a desalination process is that the thermal energy required for freezing water is   15
less than one-sixth of the heat required for evaporation. In addition, problems of corrosion or crusting are almost entirely eliminated.

[...]

PRACTICAL 13

13.3 Technical translation

**PUBLISHED TRANSLATION OF
THE SPECTROSCOPY ABSTRACT**

Text

Since Russian physicist Zavoitski performed the first Electronic Spin Resonance (ESR) experiment in 1945, this technique has reached great heights of development, comparable to those attained by Nuclear Magnetic Resonance electroscopy (NMR). This article summarizes the groups who work in Spain in ESR, as well as their lines of research. For most of them it has been and continues   5
to be a technique that is complementary to their research. Although it is a late arrival, ESR is currently becoming strongly consolidated, both with regard to equipment and to the existing critical mass.

Reprinted from Carlos Sieiro Del Nido, 'La Espectroscopía de Resonancia de Spin Electrónico (RSE) en España', in *Política Científica*, 37, (Madrid: Comisión Interministerial De Ciencia y Tecnología, 1993, p. 45), copyright © Comisión Interministerial De Ciencia y Tecnología.

Practical 14

NOTES FOR TUTORS

The first three assignments in this Practical follow a progression from cross-linguistic comparison of the parallel Kodachrome texts (on pp. 166–167 of the coursebook), through comparison of three English recipes in different styles, and of a Spanish recipe with an English recipe for a similar dish, to attempting a generically plausible translation of another Spanish recipe in class. The fourth assignment can be done independently of the others, replaced by another consumer text of the tutor's choosing, or even omitted if time is pressing.

14.1 Consumer-oriented texts

This assignment works best when prepared at home and discussed in class. Its purpose is threefold. First, it is intended to encourage students to observe textual differences, and to speculate on possible reasons for these discrepancies, between the Spanish and English versions of the Kodachrome blurb. It should be remembered that the two versions are not translations of one another but two different adaptations aimed at Spanish- and English-speaking consumers. As such, the different backgrounds, needs, and genre- related expectations of each consumer group are plausible factors in motivating textual discrepancies.

Second, the comparison asked for in the assignment invites considerations of social and tonal register. On this score, it is not so much that the register of Spanish consumer-oriented texts tends to be more formal or more peremptory than that of their English counterparts, but rather that a literal and syntactically faithful rendering of a Spanish ST *tends* to read as more stiffly formal than is normally appropriate to consumer-oriented genres in English.

The last observation points towards the third purpose of the assignment, which is to encourage students to exercise a degree of restrained freedom in producing TTs based on consumer-oriented Spanish STs. That is to say, we are recommending (within discreet limits) a style of translation that gives precedence to generic plausibility over a slavish copying of the grammar of the ST (that is, over a faithful ST-oriented translation). It is, in short, a better strategy (when translating consumer-oriented STs) to produce a user-friendly TT than to stick rigidly to the content and organization of the ST. This may imply deleting ST items that could be construed as insultingly obvious for the TL consumer, or adding details not in the ST when these are not taken for granted in the target culture, or possibly re-ordering the presentation of ideas in the TT. Such departures must, however, not be gratuitous: they must be clearly motivated by TT user-friendliness. Above all, the translator is not free to invent or distort factual information about the product.

14.2 Consumer-oriented texts

This assignment works equally well if done individually (or in groups) at home, or done in groups in class. Like the previous assignment, it is designed to foster students' awareness of genre-specific expectations. The first part of the assignment serves as a reminder that even within what is nominally a single genre (recipe book), there is, in fact, a considerable latitude and choice between different stylistic approaches (in, for instance, social and tonal register, layout, and organization). A major motivating factor for these differences is, of course, the consideration of a targeted group of consumers: a factor that one should always keep in mind when translating consumer-oriented texts. The second part of the assignment is similar to assignment 14.1, and calls attention to differences that can be expected between Spanish and English recipes in general. Among points that are likely to arise are differing stereotypical assumptions about Spanish and English consumers, about their respective approaches to shopping and cooking, and their attitudes to food as such (for example the degree of cookery skill, or the amount of time spent on cooking, considered normal in a particular culture). Some of the differences observed in the texts used here doubtless derive from the fact that the Spanish and English recipes are not translations but independently formulated texts; this makes them all the more revealing as indicators of Spanish and British expectations in respect to the genre of recipes.

14.3 Consumer-oriented texts

This assignment works well if done in groups in class. In the wake of the two previous assignments, the effect of which tends to be to remove students' inhibitions about departures from closely faithful translation of recipes, most student TTs will probably be relatively free. The problem is to decide at what point freedom becomes unwarranted licence. This is a good way of raising the question of how the demands of translation in one particular genre differ from the global requirements of a compromise between accurate and idiomatic translation in general. Discussion could usefully focus on the double purpose of user-friendliness and persuasion in consumer-oriented genres, both of which require strategic consideration of a targeted group of consumers. A good way of focusing attention on these issues is to compare possible alternative TTs ranged on a scale of decreasing literality, as are, for example, the following four TT versions of the first sentence of the ST:

(a) Whisk four egg-whites, together with a small pinch of salt, until firm peaks are formed.
(b) Whisk the whites of four eggs, together with a small pinch of salt, until they form firm peaks.
(c) 1. Add a small pinch of salt to the whites of four eggs and whisk them until they form firm peaks.
(d) Start by putting the whites of four eggs in a bowl, add a small pinch of salt, and whisk them until they are firm – you'll know they are firm enough if they stay in little peaks when you pull the whisk out.

From comparing these versions it would seem that TT (a), though accurate, is excessively terse, while TT (d) may be too patronizing; TT (b) probably best combines accuracy with idiomaticity, while TT (c) is adapted to the perceived trends of British recipe books by numbering the steps in the preparation of dishes and by reorganizing the sentential sequence to coincide with the sequence of actions (that is, first put the salt in with the egg-whites, then start whisking).

14.4 Consumer-oriented texts

This assignment is highly flexible: it probably works best as a home assignment, but it can also be done by groups concentrating on translating, and reporting on, allocated sections of the ST, or as a tutor-led class exercise with individual students contributing in turn.

The assignment provides a particularly good illustration of the need to combine, in translating consumer-oriented texts, accuracy with idiomaticity. With regard to accuracy, there are certain pitfalls for the unwary which can only be avoided by having the relevant cultural and factual information. In this respect, the assignment bears a surprising similarity to technical translation. There are, however, also a number of specifically consumer-oriented considerations to take into account: an idiomatic and user-friendly style, in keeping with genre-specific expectations; an appropriate, friendly but not unduly patronizing, register aimed at a plausible group of tourists; and elements of persuasion which make a tour of Santo Domingo sound interesting and attractive.

Practical 15

NOTES FOR TUTORS

15.1 Stylistic editing

Students should be asked to prepare this assignment for discussion in class. Their initial response may be somewhat inhibited and reluctant, tinged by the feeling that they have been set an unreasonable task. They may argue, with some justification, that the TTs cannot be edited without access to the relevant STs. Had they been asked to make *final* editing decisions, they would, of course, be entirely correct in this judgement. However, our point is that, ideally, a TT should, at some stage in the translation process, be assessed without consultation of the ST. Translators are not well placed to carry out this operation on their own TTs, because they are unavoidably influenced by their knowledge of the ST. The task is best carried out by a competent TL reader who has no access to the ST. It is in this capacity that students are asked to edit the texts in this assignment: not in order to make final editing decisions, but to call into question points in the TTs that seem infelicitous to them, and to make tentative suggestions for emendations. It is worth reminding students that this is a valuable contribution to the translation process, and involves a realistic task for working translators, not a merely academic exercise. (Apart from its own intrinsic value, this assignment also serves as a preliminary warm-up exercise for the following assignment.)

15.2 Stylistic editing

This is a fairly time-consuming assignment designed for group work in class. Parts (i) and (ii), which go hand in hand, must be completed speedily (in not more than half an hour, including discussion), so as to leave sufficient time for Part (iii) and for ample class discussion of final editing decisions. The elimination of obvious infelicities from the TT, some of which can be done before the ST is handed out to students, is relatively easy. Final editing can, of course, only be carried out by reference to the ST given on pp. 102–103 below.

PRACTICAL 15

15.2 Stylistic editing

ST OF THE EXTRACT FROM
COLOMBIA: PAÍS DE ELDORADO

Text

COLOMBIA

PAÍS DE ELDORADO

Cuando el territorio que hoy ocupa Colombia comenzó a ser conquistado por los españoles en el siglo XVI nació una leyenda: Eldorado... fabuloso tesoro que se suponía escondido en el fondo de todas las aguas, enterrado en todos los socavones, tropezado en cada mina.... 5

Sin embargo, los conquistadores no pudieron localizar aquella inmensa riqueza cuya sola descripción exaltaba los ánimos e infundía valor aún en los cobardes....

Los conquistadores no sabían que no todo lo que brilla es oro y que no todos los tesoros pueden ser sometidos a acuñación: el tesoro saltaba a la vista, estaba a 10 flor de tierra:... eran los climas el tesoro, los frutos generosos, los cielos abiertos, las llanuras, y montañas: Colombia, era Eldorado....

Por eso, este país situado en el extremo norte de la América del Sur es indescriptible con el lenguaje usado en las publicaciones de turismo. Para hablar de él hay que dejarse poseer por la pasión, recurrir al lenguaje que utilizan los 15 inventores de leyendas....

Seguramente usted leyó Cien Años de Soledad, aquella novela tan famosa del colombiano García Márquez, donde las muchachas vuelan y los muertos permanecen atados a los árboles o deambulan por las casonas....

...Bueno, pues ya tiene usted una idea aproximada de lo que es este país 20 misterioso... lleno de sueños de imposibilidad... De Colombia, crea todo lo que le digan... Este es un país excesivo. Nuestro territorio es ya una sorprendente manifestación de plenitud: costas en dos océanos, selvas impenetrables [algunas de ellas con aeropuerto], tres enormes cordilleras y grandes ríos que alimentan poblaciones innumerables.... 25

Colombia ha sido llamado también país de ciudades... Tenemos muchas... Pequeñas, apacibles, tradicionalistas, llenas de reliquias históricas, unas... Y otras, modernas, del siglo veinte, lanzadas al torrente vertiginoso del progreso... Pero todas unidas por muy buenas carreteras y vías férreas y eficientes conexiones aéreas.... 30

Practicals 16–19

NOTES FOR TUTORS

Contrastive topics

As explained on pp. 185–186 of the coursebook, each of the chapters on contrastive topics is self-contained, and may be inserted at whatever point in the course tutors find most appropriate. We do not consider them any more lightweight, conceptually or practically, than Chapters 1–15, but they do provide a different sort of work from those chapters, and they make for a different sort of class. As a result, they provide a change of pace which students may find refreshing. One possibility, then, is to tackle a contrastive topic every five weeks or so. Of course, local factors may suggest departures from such a neat scheme. The 'wild card' value of these classes is enhanced by two further factors. First, Chapters 18 and 19 can either be paired together or used separately as half-classes in conjunction with the work from one of the earlier chapters. Second, none of these practicals, if prepared by students in advance, is likely to take up an entire two-hour class; consequently, the remaining time can be given over to completing any of the speed translations that may have been squeezed out of earlier practicals by pressure of time. Although the contrastive chapters are self-contained, there are very many links between them and the rest of the material in the book. It is a good idea for tutors to call attention to these links wherever appropriate – cross-references will, of course, depend on the order in which the topics are covered.

The aims and methods of the contrastive chapters are explained in each. There is no need to go over them again here, save to stress that *each preliminary exercise must be completed before the relevant chapter is read*. We should also stress that, like all the others, these practicals must be thoroughly prepared by students in advance of the class: the expository material needs to be properly digested; the examples need to be thought about in readiness for discussion, and those for which no translation is given should be translated. Class discussion should be as lively for these four chapters as for any of the others. For our part, we lay no more claim here than in the rest of the course to having found *the* explanations and *the* solutions: tutors and students are as certain here as in the rest of the course to disagree constructively with us and among themselves.